Your CORE Strength

A young woman's go-to guide to **eating**, **exercise**, and **empowered health**.

AMY CONNELL

I am not a doctor, physical therapist, or registered dietician. The content provided herein is simply for educational purposes and does not take the place of medical advice from your provider. Every effort has been made to ensure that the content provided in this book is accurate and helpful for my readers at the time of publication. However, this is not an exhaustive treatment of the subjects. No liability is assumed for losses or damages due to the information provided. You are responsible for your own choices, actions, and results. You should consult your personal medical professional for specific problems.

All scripture is from THE HOLY BIBLE, NEW INTERNATIONAL VERSION®, NIV® Copyright © 1973, 1978, 1984, 2011 by Biblica, Inc.® unless otherwise noted. Used by permission. All rights reserved worldwide.

Paperback ISBN: 978-1-7377076-4-6
E-book ISBN: 978-1-7377076-5-3

Copyright © 2024 Amy Connell LLC

Visit the author's website at www.gracedhealth.com

Cover and Interior design by KUHN Design Group | kuhndesigngroup.com
Photo by Katherine Suzette

All rights reserved. No portion of this book may be reproduced in any form without permission from the publisher, except as permitted by U.S. copyright law.

For permissions contact: amy.connell@gracedhealth.com

Applause from Young Women

This book is an incredible and entertaining source of positivity, encouragement, and relief for girls who feel like they have to fit certain criteria of body image and reach absurd statistics of diet culture to feel like they're enough (Spoiler: you don't!). Reading this took a huge weight off my shoulders as someone who spent her teenage years, and a bit before that, comparing herself, criticizing her own weight, and constantly being in her head about what she looked like. *Your CORE Strength* helped me realize that is not what life's about and that there's so much more in store for us to strive for and achieve than a number on a scale!

Jenna, age 19

Your CORE Strength is the perfect guide for teenage girls to navigate the modern expectations of what it means to be healthy and to understand the true meaning behind physical and spiritual health. I am so grateful for the new perspectives this book holds, and love how applicable it is to the time we are living in!

Ella, age 18

Your CORE Strength is an incredible book for young women who are seeking guidance in their health journey. It provides a knowledgeable approach, tackling topics of physical, emotional, and mental well-being in today's society. I enjoyed the plethora of tips and tricks included in the book and cannot wait to implement them into my everyday life!

Alyssa, age 18

Your CORE Strength helped me build and work on my relationship with healthy habits and a positive mindset. It helps reinforce the love and joy you should feel with your body's purpose and builds one's strength by having this knowledge. Amy's book fills you with confidence and comfort in who you are and what your body's purpose is.

Amelie, age 17

Your CORE Strength taught me that it doesn't matter what my weight is or if I constantly exercise. It taught me to listen to my body and eat what makes me feel good. I liked *Your CORE Strength* because it showed me that there is no good food or bad food. It was totally different than what I was expecting!

Hannah, age 14

I like that *Your CORE Strength* was a faith-based book on how to be healthy and surprised to find that it wasn't about how to eat well-balanced meals and snacks. I liked the tips on how to exercise and the different ways to exercise.

Abigail, age 17

Praise from the Experts

As a mom to three daughters, this resource is a wealth of information and inspiration for the entire family. Amy Connell explores the multifaceted nature of health and gives teens the tools to incorporate these concepts into daily life. As a therapist, I appreciate the introduction of a shared vocabulary upon which mothers and daughters can connect and grow.

Kate Casey LPC, JD

Amy Connell has a gift for making our health goals practical and manageable. Her book, *Your CORE Strength* eases the pressure so many feel to go on extreme diets or workout plans, and offers practical steps of moderation to attain a healthy mind and body. Amy's humor mixed with up-to-date research and personal coaching experience, makes it hard to put the book down! You will feel understood and cared for by both a professional and a caring "big sister!"

Sue Corl, Executive Director of Crown of Beauty International, *His Heartbeat Podcast*, and author of *Crown of Beauty 12-week Women's Bible study*.

Now more than ever teen girls need encouragement and straight talk to help them cut through the noise around health, exercise, and eating. Amy Connell touches on an extensive list of topics with expertise, grace, and a thorough understanding of how tough it is to be a girl in this culture. Amy's words will be a burst of biblical truth and relatable sanity that soothes a teen girl's soul in a world that's too often mixed up about how to be healthy.

Heather Creekmore, Podcast host and author of four books including *The 40-Day Body Image Workbook: Help for Christian Women Who've Tried Everything*

With wisdom and wit, Amy offers solid, grace-filled guidance for young women—and really, women of all ages—in finding ways to feel and function well. *Your CORE Strength* is an essential partner for anyone who desires to care for their health without the rules and confusion of constantly shifting body ideals and fad diets.

Lisa DeKam, Physical Therapist, Founder of The Axia Project

What an easy read, packed with so much power! When it comes to health, Amy debunks common health myths and breaks down the truth! It's not about "good" versus "bad," that's diet culture! Instead, she gives the 411 on eating right, sleeping well, and honoring our God-given bodies. This book is a tool I wish I had ten years ago, instead of unlearning and relearning myself!

Chelsea Haynes, TV Host

In a world where teens are taught that how you look determines your value, *Your CORE Strength* teaches a balanced, faith-based, and mentally healthy approach regarding health and wellness for girls.

Michelle Nietert, M.A., LPC-S, Clinical Director of Hope Helps, Author of six books including *Managing Your Emojis, Make Up Your Mind*, and *Bringing Big Emotions to a Bigger God* series including *God, I Feel Sad/Scared*.

In this transformative book, Amy continues her crusade against diet culture and challenges the predominant beliefs about what it is to be "healthy." As a woman, a mother of two young women, and a therapist, I am only too aware of how this culture has, and continues to, ruined the internal narrative women have about themselves and others. *Your CORE Strength* provides expert guidance and actionable tips to teenage girls on how to pursue the kind of health that really matters. Amy challenges us all to embrace our God-given unique bodies and to consider how He calls us to fulfill his purposes for us.

Ruth Opiyo, Psychotherapist, MA LPC

I wish I would have read this book 20 years ago! *Your CORE Strength* is an invaluable resource for teen girls. Amy uses a biblical worldview to emphasize the importance of feeling and functioning well while debunking the many lies of diet culture. She shares helpful insight with readers regarding health and fitness while reminding them that their worth is not found in these things. Amy writes with knowledge, truth, and humor and will leave you feeling like you're chatting over coffee with a friend!

Kristin Williams, RDN, LD, CEDS

Your CORE Strength is a guide for Christian girls who want to know what it means to be healthy. Amy doesn't mince words and gets straight to the point, leaving no rocks unturned when it comes to the foundations of health being rooted in God alongside big-picture principles for the body. She is conversational and kind throughout. You can tell she's not only a mom, but has a mother's heart for every girl she addresses in this book. As a non-diet Christian health coach, I fully recommend this guide for both health-seeking Christian girls and their parents. We no longer need to conform to the ways of culture, but to define health by the gospel. This book is an important step in the right direction!

Kasey Shuler, co-founder of Joyful Health Co.
and author of *Move for Joy*

This is a resource I wish I had as a teen! *Your CORE Strength* is the perfect book for pre-teens and teens who want to learn how to get healthy without it feeling like an impossible goal. As a Jesus-loving dietitian, I love how Amy presents tangible ways to add positive health behaviors into day-to-day life without it being tied to diet culture. The best part is how she presents health from a Biblical perspective that is not just a verse being slapped onto another ineffective diet plan. If you want to get a healthy, heart, mind, and body without a bunch of nonsense, this book is for you.

Brittany Wilson, RDN, Certified Intuitive Eating Counselor

For the young women who have already trusted me with their
bodies through my guidance about food and exercise,
and for those who will trust me with their bodies
by reading my guidance in this book.

*I pray you feel the abundant love of the Creator
who made your beautiful, original body.*

Author's Note

Your CORE Strength is intended for informational and educational purposes only. If you are struggling with an eating disorder or any mental health issue, please seek professional help. *Your CORE Strength* is not a substitute for professional advice, diagnosis, or treatment. Your health and well-being are paramount, and it's important to prioritize seeking help from qualified professionals who can provide personalized support and guidance tailored to your individual needs. Remember, you are not alone, and there are resources available to assist you on your journey to recovery. If you don't know where to begin, I offer several resources throughout this book or you can visit NationalEatingDisorders.org.

CONTENTS

Introduction 15

PART ONE: WARM UP

1. What Is My CORE Strength? 23
2. C—What Is My Calling? 27
3. O—How Can I Celebrate My Originality? 33
4. R—Why Are Relationships Important to My Health? ... 39
5. How Can I Set Boundaries in My Relationships? 47
6. E—What Does It Mean to Take Care of Myself? 51
7. How Do I Know If I'm Healthy? 57

PART TWO: WORK OUT

8. How Can I Take Care of My Mental Health? 65
9. How Do I Sleep Better? 73
10. What Do You Mean There Are No "Good" and "Bad" Foods? 81
11. What Does "Diet Culture" Mean? 85
12. What Foods Help My Body Feel Good? 89
13. How Do I Nourish Myself? 99
14. How Can I Drink More Water? 103
15. How Much Protein Do I Need? 107
16. What's the Deal with Fats? 111
17. Are Carbs Bad for Me? 115
18. Is Sugar Bad for Me? 123

19. Will I Gain Weight If I Eat Sweet Foods? 129
20. What's the Right Way to Eat? 133
21. How Should I Warm Up? 139
22. How Do I Create a Workout That's Best for Me? 143
23. Why Should I Strength Train? 149
24. How Do I Strengthen My Core? 155
25. How Long Should I Work Out? 161
26. Why Do I Throw Up During or After My Workout? 165
27. How Should I Cool Down? 171
28. Why Do I Need a Rest Day? What Should I Do? 175
29. Why Can't I Poop? 181
30. How Can I Lose Weight? Should I? Do I Need To? 187

PART THREE: COOL DOWN

31. How Do I Know If I'm Successful at Being Healthy? 201
32. A Quick Note about Your Mom from a Mom 205
33. How Do I Break Free from Comparison? 211
34. I Feel and Function Well. Is That It? 215

Conclusion 219
What's Next? 223
Resource Guide 225
Recipes 241
Acknowledgments 267
Notes 279

INTRODUCTION

What comes to mind when you hear the word "health?"

If you want to roll your eyes because you're so tired of hearing that word, you're in luck.

If you love learning about healthy living, you're in luck.

If you wish you knew more but are overwhelmed by all the dos and don'ts, you're in luck.

Or maybe you're like me when I listen to my sons talk about physics. I get simple physics concepts like "gravity causes an apple to fall from the tree," and I often quote that an object in motion stays in motion, but if you bring up derivatives, diffraction, and dynamics, my eyes gloss over.

Physics can be confusing. Figuring out how to be healthy can be confusing too. There's so much out there. Where do we even start?

You're in luck: I'm here to clarify the confusion about healthy living and answer the questions I get the most as a personal trainer and nutrition coach.

What you'll get out of reading this book:

- » Science-backed information to empower you to take care of yourself
- » A new way of thinking about *why* we take care of ourselves
- » Encouragement to figure out what is best for you at the right time for you
- » Answers to some of the most common questions I've received from people of all ages throughout my fitness career

What you won't get out of reading this book:

- » A list of one-size-fits-all rules that are difficult to achieve and more difficult to sustain
- » Expectations of perfection
- » Food, body, or any other kind of shaming

How to read this book

- » **Read Part One first.** This will be the foundation of all we talk about. Before we get into the specifics about food and exercise, I want to make sure you understand where I'm coming from. And I want us beside each other the whole way through.
- » **Choose your own adventure in Part Two.** I'm giving you permission right here, right now to jump around and read the Part Two chapters you're most interested in. Obviously, I hope you read them all at some point, and you'll get bonus points if you read them in order, but it's not required.

» **Finish with Part Three.** It's a wrap-up of all we'll discuss, and it will guide you through some of the heavier questions you may have.

» **Access the resources at the end of the book.** Throughout Part Two, I offer suggestions for recipes and workouts. Those recipes and YouTube links to the workouts are all in the Resource Guide.

Why did I write this book?

Quite honestly, it's something I wish I had growing up.

I wish:

» Someone had planted a new seed in me that told me that my eating, exercise, and body didn't have to be "perfect"

» Someone would have encouraged me to be kind to myself

» I had learned to give myself grace

It's also a need I've seen in working with teen fitness clients for the last five years. Each summer, I've led strength and conditioning classes and taught a simple nutrition lesson at the end of each class. I noticed neighborhood high schoolers exercising on their own and going to local gyms. I wanted to teach them proper form and provide a positive environment as the foundation for their relationship with working out. My smart, kind clients also felt overwhelmed and confused by all the "food rules" out there. I wanted to provide applicable, sustainable and truthful nutrition. I aim to do all of that for you in this book as well.

In a noisy, chaotic world full of influencers trying to sell you programs and products in sixty-second clips, this book turns down the volume to a peaceful level — and the gentle, science-backed guidance here will last much longer than anything in your quickly moving feed.

Back to my first question about health...

Before we get started: when I say the word "health," please know that *health isn't about looking a certain way.* It's not a list of dos and don'ts. It's not a static adjective like "hot," "fit," or "perfect." It's a fluid, dynamic attitude rather than an objective scorecard.

I liken the word "health" to one of the Greek words for "love" in the Bible: *agape.* *Agape* love is unconcerned with the self and concerned with the greatest good of another.

What if we swapped the word *agape* for "health" in that definition?

Health is unconcerned with the self and concerned with the greatest good of another. This doesn't mean that we're not concerned about our own health at all, or that we need to care for others at the expense of our own health. Rather, it means that our health is less concerned with how we look and more about being physically equipped to love others. If this sounds strange, stick with me as we dig into the meaning behind CORE Strength.

Wait, what does God have to do with our health?

We will get into this throughout Part One, but in a nutshell, my faith in Jesus drives everything I do and has been instrumental in how I view my health and body differently than I used to. You'll see that my story and perspective is presented through the lens of my faith, but no matter how (or if) faith is part of your story, there is room for you in these pages. You are welcome on this journey even if we don't see eye to eye on everything.

I am so glad you are here!

You have no idea how much I mean that. I feel like my nearly twenty years as a fitness professional, certification as a nutrition coach, and work with young women has led me to this.

A few years ago, I flippantly asked God why He never allowed me to have the visible six-pack abs I so desperately wanted. His answer? "Because you wouldn't be able to do what you're doing now."

I believe God gave me two boys to care for as a parent because he knew I'd be loving you girls in this other way—by coming to you as part mentor, part coach, and part quirky aunt who calls it like it is, even when it's awkward. I so wish we could discuss this over Starbucks, or better yet, on a walk-and-talk (you'll hear more about those later). Since we can't, stick this book in your bag and know that my heart is with you.

Ready? Let's dig into science and scripture to discover the grace and freedom God has for you. And yes, you can grab a little chocolate for the trip. I'll be enjoying Dove dark chocolate and almond, but you can get your favorite.

Part One

WARM UP

Just like our bodies need to warm up to get the most out of a workout, in this section, we are going to warm up our minds.

Full disclosure—throughout this book, I'll be asking you to think differently. It may feel weird at first, but then your brain will get used to it, kind of like the first time you walk through the halls of a new school. It's awkward and strange, but soon enough, you get comfortable.

I promise I'll get to the nitty-gritty questions about exercise and eating later on. But first, I want to explore the ways we think about our bodies, how we define health, and why we even want to be healthy in the first place.

Pull up your favorite playlist and cue the music. Let's go!

Chapter 1

WHAT IS MY CORE STRENGTH?

What do you think of math? We all have different experiences with learning math, but I've found that people often fall into two camps: love it or hate it. Me? I enjoy it. Some of it is the way my brain works, and some of it is from my dad's dinnertime training growing up.

My dad, mom, younger sister, and I would sit around the dinner table engaging in normal conversation. My dad would be in the middle of a story discussing how gas had increased 15% from $2 a gallon, and then his eyes would jump to me and he'd say, "so what is it now?"

Math on the fly—that's what every eighth-grader loves to do while eating chicken parmesan. But I learned to quickly calculate figures, which is *super* helpful as a personal trainer. (Note my sarcasm. Thankfully, this quick math *did* help in my first career as a financial analyst!)

I didn't get it then, but my dad was teaching me the foundations of using math in everyday life.

We've all had foundational classes in math, beginning in kindergarten with simple calculations like 1+1=2. Each year, our understanding and knowledge grows as we learn more complicated ways of practicing math. (Fourth-grade long division had me in tears, but that's beside the point.) We grow from understanding the basics to learning and applying more in our algebra, geometry, and possibly even calculus classes.

Think of this first section as our 1+1=2 understanding of why we take care of ourselves. Our CORE Strength is the foundation of everything we will discuss in this book.

Before we get into the details of taking care of ourselves, I want to give you some underlying truths. These may be different from what you've heard or seen before, and I'm okay with that. I'm calling this primary work our CORE Strength.

So what is our CORE Strength?

I've created an acronym to help us remember, and I'll be referencing it throughout the book.

C—**Calling:** We take care of ourselves so we can do what we are called to do.

O—**Originality:** Our body is a gift from God, original and unique.

R—**Relationships:** We take care of ourselves so we can enjoy and engage in relationships with God and with one another.

E—**Everything:** Everything counts in our health journeys, not just food and fitness.

Our CORE Strength is this: We take care of our original bodies in a variety of ways so we can do what we are called to do.

By the way, if you read this chapter title and expected exercises to give you six-pack abs, I'm sorry to disappoint you. But don't worry; we will talk about strengthening our core muscles later. Our CORE Strength is the foundation of why we take care of ourselves. Spoiler alert: it's not so we can look a certain way. It's so we can be confident in how we feel and function in all areas of our lives. Our CORE Strength sets us up for success so we can be the best women we can be, now and in the future. And that lasts longer than even the most shredded six-pack abs!

We take care of our original bodies in a variety of ways so we can do what we are called to do.

Chapter 2

C – WHAT IS MY CALLING?

Several years ago, I was speaking to a group of cheerleaders at a local Christian high school. They were celebrating the nearing end of the school year with brunch and anticipating sleeping in during the summer months. They just had to get through two more days of final exams and they'd be home free.

Over our cinnamon rolls and breakfast casserole, I asked, "I'm curious... what do you feel your calling is?"

Crickets.

Inside, I panicked a little, because it seemed like my question didn't land particularly well. But outside, I smiled wider and said, "surely someone here has something they want to do in the future?"

One young woman spoke up. Her glazed eyes indicated she'd been up late studying and felt stressed.

"Honestly," she said, "right now I just want to pass my chemistry final."

Multiple heads nodded in agreement.

Fair enough. Even though questions about what you want to do after high school seem to come before you even *start* high school, it can be hard to see past the next pressing moment. Exams, athletic games, theater productions, and more are always coming one right after the other, and it's difficult to think beyond each new thing.

But what exactly is a *calling*? How do we know what ours is? And how does that fit into the zillions of other things we have to do each day?

The Bible doesn't provide a definition for "calling" or "purpose," but considering the Ten Commandments and what we learn from Jesus, I believe a calling centers around *using our God-given talents and gifts to glorify God and to love and serve others.*

Let's explore some of the ways God may be asking us to use our bodies to love and serve others.

Micro callings

Little daily callings; moments and opportunities to love and serve others

Let's revisit that chemistry exam. Pretend this young woman had hopes of becoming a nurse. She needs to do well in her high school science classes to impress college admissions counselors. Doing well on this chemistry exam is a micro calling. Health-wise, she needs to get enough sleep and eat foods that give her mental clarity to get a good grade.

Other micro callings might be:

> » Reaching out to a friend just to let her know you're thinking of her
> » Playing our best in an important soccer match
> » Inviting a friend to youth group
> » Tutoring a classmate who is struggling

Creative callings

Using the intricacies of how God made you to bless others and fill your own soul

Do you doodle? Paint? Write? Bake and decorate unique cookies? Make encouraging Reels? Capture beauty behind the lens of a camera?

If so, you're using the creativity God gave you, and I bet those gifts are blessing others. Don't discount your gifts. Creative work of any type fills our souls when we see or experience it. When you create, you're giving others a glimpse of God's glory.

We certainly can't discount how sacred creativity is to God. If you doubt that, step outside and watch the sunrise or sunset. Take notice of the colorful butterflies, birds, or plants. Peek outside an airplane window (or look up a gorgeous photograph of a thirty-thousand-foot view) and observe the landscape. God's creative hand is evident in all of nature, just waiting to bless us. Look for inventive ways to bless others to experience this calling.

Service callings

Serving others with our time, care, or presence

In other words, these callings are about being a friend to someone who needs some support. Sometimes God asks us to help fulfill someone else's calling.

> » My friends support me by texting me words of encouragement
>
> » I helped my neighbor who was out of town by checking on her house and watering her plants
>
> » When my sons' friends show up at their basketball games or track meets, it's incredibly meaningful (to them and to me)

How can you serve others? Look around at neighbors, friends, and classmates. See if there's an opportunity, big or small, to help someone out.

Seasonal callings

A calling for a period of time

Sometimes God wants us to focus on something for a period of time, and then He pivots us to something else. It may be a clear path, or it may feel like a blindfolded pin-the-tail-on-the-donkey step of faith. When we walk with God, we never know where He will take us or how long we will be there.

I like to say I'm in Phase Three of my adult life. Right after I graduated college, I joined the corporate world and used my finance degree. When my husband and I started a family, we both decided that I would stay home with our boys. After several years, I felt God calling me into writing and speaking about His health vs. the world's view of health.

So far, I've had three seasonal callings. I will probably have more in the future. I don't know what those will be, but I do know that I trust God when He asks me to do something different, even when it's scary or uncomfortable.

You may or may not be able to point to seasonal callings in your life right now, but you'll probably be able to look back later and identify what falls into this category. This is also a good reminder that it's okay if things change … it may be a seasonal calling. Stay connected with God and He will guide you in the next steps.

Macro callings
Larger-scale plans

Macro callings are what we often think of when we hear the word "calling" or "purpose."

If you've read the biblical book of Exodus, you may remember reading about how Moses grew from a shepherd tending to his flock to a prophet convincing Pharaoh to free the Israelites from slavery in Egypt. Moses only did this because God spoke to him through a bush that was on fire but not burning down to ashes. Talk about a macro calling!

Maybe God won't appear to you through a flaming bush, but have you ever gotten that fire in your heart that you are meant to do something big?

- » Lead a small group at your house
- » Babysit regularly for a struggling family
- » Start a student organization at your school
- » Write a book

Has your heart ever burned for an issue or a cause? What keeps you up at night? If you can't identify a macro calling right now, don't worry. I bet right now God has you focusing on the other types of callings we've already talked about. But keep your heart open and your eyes on the horizon for any large-scale callings He may be preparing for you.

«»

Despite what you've heard, your body is not here to look a certain way (more on this in the next chapter). Our bodies are given to us to glorify God, love and serve others, and fulfill the many types of callings God gives us. Our bodies should honor God and His desires for us in all we do. (Or we should at least try. Lord knows I don't live up to it all the time.)

As for our callings, they can change. Some are big and some are small. Some are long-term and some are short-term. And sometimes we think our calling is one thing, but it turns out to be something different than we anticipated. All of these are normal. But one thing they all have in common: our bodies need to be prepared for whatever God has for us.

Chapter 3

O – HOW CAN I CELEBRATE MY ORIGINALITY?

When you look in the mirror, how do you see yourself? How do you feel about your body?

This might be a *very* loaded question for you. I've gone through various responses to these questions throughout my own life. In some seasons, I've found acceptance and dare I say—pride. But in far too many seasons, I've felt somewhere on the spectrum between unhappy, discouraged, and ashamed.

Why is it so challenging to accept our bodies? Volumes of books have been written attempting to answer this question, but I think it comes down to this: *we have a hard time celebrating the originality God created in all of us.*

How can you celebrate your original body?

Consider the three Gs:

God's original design is evident in your unique body

If you've grown up in the church, you're probably familiar with Genesis 1:27: "God created mankind in his own image." You may have heard Psalm 139:14 as well: "I praise you because I am fearfully and wonderfully made; your works are wonderful, I know that full well."

May I be honest? I still have a hard time wrapping my brain around that. How am I made in the image of God when everyone on earth looks so different from each other and they're all made in His image as well? But it's like the physics homework my son does: just because I don't understand it doesn't mean it's not true.

Have you ever seen a parent introduce their new baby? Their wide smiles and shining eyes show their love for their child. Or maybe you remember having a younger sibling you were so proud to hold and meet? This is a fraction of the pride God takes in each of us.

God specifically designed my unique body. Yours, too. He has a plan and purpose for each of our bodies, which is why He tasks us with taking care of them. If He wanted our bodies to look taller, shorter, leaner, or juicier (probably not a term God uses, but you never know), then He would have made them that way.

Your differences are evidence of God's original design. Imagine your favorite Netflix show. Now think about what that show would be like if the cast of characters were all basically the same. Their genders, personalities, and even physical characteristics were identical. Pretty boring, huh? Their differences working together is what draws us to the stories they act out.

God made our differences as a full cast of characters. And He designed our original bodies on purpose for a purpose within His script of life.

Genetics play an uncontrollable factor

I recently went on a trip with my sister and our husbands. We were both tickled by how many people asked if we were sisters. But for all the physical similarities we have, we also have differences.

Genetics play a huge role in our physical appearances. If you've been through a basic biology class, you probably already know this. Some genes, such as the ones that decide eye color and skin tone, are easy to see. Others, like the ones that control bone density and metabolic differences, are not.

Your parents gave you a unique set of characteristics. I can point out my husband's frame in one of my sons and my nose in the other. You may have your mom's eyes, dad's skin tone, and grandma's smile. Even if you don't know everything about your family history, you carry your ancestors' genetic history.

Families that come together through adoption create a beautiful mix of nature and nurture. You may not be fully aware of your genetics, but you are shaped by the God-designed family you are in. The unique values and dynamics that are imparted to you through family members and peers play a huge role as well. How your family celebrates, worships, eats, moves, relaxes, and vacations all contribute to the way you relate to the world.

When my kids were little and complained about what I chose for them to watch on TV, I would tell them, "you get what you get and you don't throw a fit." Sometimes I wonder if God wants to say that to us when we complain about the unique and original characteristics He specifically gave each of our bodies.

Glory-filled cultures are different...and they still change

Have you ever learned about what is considered "beautiful" by cultures other than your own? Not all cultures have the same body ideal. As a white woman, I can't claim to be the authority on this, but the area where I live is one of the most diverse counties in the country. When I asked a multi-ethnic Facebook group of women in my community what is traditionally considered beautiful and desirable by their culture of origin, the answers varied as far as the world is round.

I heard from Chinese women who desired a "soft" and slim body; Latinas who looked for curves and long, thick, wavy hair; Indian women who were obsessed with big eyes with beautiful lashes and eyebrows and not being skinny; and Nigerians who desired long legs, big butts, and wide hips. Additionally, I've learned that African American women's body image doesn't begin and end with size as it often does for white women. For some Black women, a bigger body might demonstrate health and strength, and studies show that Black women are more accepting of a wider range of body shapes.[1]

Throughout American history, the definition of beauty has constantly been in flux—and if we aren't careful, it takes our confidence along for the bumpy ride.

Want proof? Consider the "ideal" American body during these time periods:

- 1920s: flat chest; downplayed waist; bobbed hair; boyish figure
- 1930s–1950s: curves; hourglass figure; large breasts; slim waist (think pinup girls)
- 1960s: willowy; thin; long, slim legs; adolescent physique
- 1980s: athletic; svelte but curvy; tall; toned arms
- 1990s: waifish; extremely thin; translucent skin; androgynous
- 2000s to today: flat stomach; "healthy" skinny; tan; large breasts and butts; thigh gaps[2]

I go into more depth in my first book, *Your Worthy Body*, if you'd like to read more. I hope you get the point, though; our cultures of origin may impact how we feel about our bodies, but it's not the same for everyone. Since every culture is created and blessed by God, our unique bodies can confidently glorify Him, no matter how we grew up or where we came from.

The world is fickle. If we let it determine whether we feel good about how we look, we'll never keep up. Besides, why should we strive for an "ideal" body when God never says there is one, regardless of culture? This is why we have to keep revisiting our truth: we were uniquely made by God on purpose for a purpose.

As cheesy as it sounds, you truly are an original. Celebrate it!

Chapter 4

R – WHY ARE RELATIONSHIPS IMPORTANT TO MY HEALTH?

How did life change for you during the height of the COVID-19 pandemic? At a minimum, you probably learned how to use Zoom or another online video platform. In the blink of an eye, we were all taken away from our friends, classmates, teammates, churches, and more. As hard as everyone tried, online education was a bust, and seeing friends over FaceTime wasn't the same as real life.

About two weeks after the lockdown began, my college girlfriends and I officially canceled our annual trip. We are spread throughout the country and try hard to see each other in person once a year. I know there were much more serious issues our country was dealing with at the time, but I couldn't stop crying the day we canceled. My friends, both near and far, mean the world to me. And a Zoom meetup just wasn't the same.

Relationships matter. If you're wondering how this conversation fits into a health-focused book, hang with me. Let's talk about two areas of relationships that are critical to healthy mindsets and lifestyles.

1. Relationship with God

I will be the first to tell you that even as I write about all things health, I am not perfect at all things health. Sometimes I don't fully pay attention to what I'm eating and find myself overfull. I don't always get a workout in. And from time to time, I still struggle with what I see in the mirror.

But even on those days I struggle, I can still lean into my relationship with God. (By the way, this goes for days you might struggle with God in general. He's not afraid of your doubts and dark thoughts, so try telling Him about those feelings.) If I don't have God guiding my steps each day, I have no idea where I'm going. This is the vertical relationship that's critical to me. It's not a list of dos and don'ts and earning my way to eternal life. Rather, it's knowing that God delights in me and has a plan and purpose for me, even if I don't know what that is.

There's no recipe or formula to growing in this relationship. Reading His Word in the Bible is helpful. So is just talking to God like you would talk to your best friend. Making time and space to do this helps you hear Him. It's hard to hear God's whispers when everything around us is so noisy.

> **Pro Tip:** *Not sure where to begin in the Bible? Start with the book of John. It's a great account of Jesus's life and lets you see Him in action as the loving person He was.*

God delights in me and has a plan and purpose for me, even if I don't know what that is.

Staying close to God helps you hold on to a healthy perspective about your health. When I approach my health through the lens of my CORE Strength and my relationship with the One who created me rather than through the lens of the latest Instagram ad, I'm more focused, centered, and peaceful—and I can better focus on all of the other aspects of my CORE Strength.

2. Relationships with others

Why was I so, so weepy when my friends and I canceled our trip because of COVID? In hindsight, I can see how lonely I was. I couldn't see any of my friends in person. I missed hugs and laughter and confiding in trusted friends. But I wasn't alone. And even if you've felt lonely, pandemic or no pandemic, you're not alone.

Some reports state that Gen Z is the loneliest age group and that 65% of Gen Z "Zoomers" sometimes or always feel lonely.[1]

What does this have to do with our health? Loneliness is a one-two punch, attacking both your mental and physical health. In fact, being lonely can have similar effects to being an alcoholic or smoking fifteen cigarettes per day.[2] Yikes.

But here's the problem: good friends can be hard to find. Sure, you may have your ride-or-dies that have been with you since you were all in diapers, but those can be few and far between. Middle school seems to shake up friendships, then rinse and repeat when you begin high school and after you graduate. A friend of mine once said, "anyone who has been through middle school has experienced low-grade trauma." I'm raising my hand over here remembering the time I found a wad of spit in my hair, and I think you may be raising your hand as well for your own reasons. (I really hope you never found spit in your hair. That was *so* gross and embarrassing.)

Relationships with others are the horizontal relationships we reach out to, rather than the vertical relationship we have with God, whom we look up to.

How can we create trusted horizontal relationships? Here are a few ideas to get you going:

- » *Friends need to earn each other's trust.* Start with small things ("oh my gosh, I snorted while laughing about genes versus jeans in biology today!") before moving on to the big things ("I'm really struggling and feel depressed").
- » *Find activities where you're doing something side by side.* Personally, I love walks with friends because it can feel awkward to look someone in the eye for an entire conversation. I call these "walk-and-talks." Some of my closest in-person friendships have developed on the sidewalks of my neighborhood.
- » *Reach out* to a teammate you enjoy practicing with and see if they want to work on drills, or to a fellow theater friend to run lines. The one-on-one or small-group time is a good way to get to know each other better.
- » *Faith-based small groups* can be a great place to connect and cut through the superficial stuff. Ask your youth group leader if they have any groups you can join … or, better yet, start your own with a Bible study and a leader guide!

If you're not plugged into a church, explore apps like the YouVersion Bible or Minted Truth. You can even grab the discussion guide to this book (link in the Resource Guide) and go through it with a few friends.

» There is a time and place for online friendships, but let those supplement your in-person friendships rather than replace them. If you have good, trusted friends who have moved, though, keep in touch! Some of my closest friendships are those I made in college. We live all over the country but connect via walk-and-talks and texts.

This is a good time to acknowledge that not all friendships and relationships are unicorns and rainbows. (Again... middle school trauma is real.) It takes time for anyone to develop deep, meaningful relationships.

What do we get when we intersect our vertical relationship with our horizontal ones?

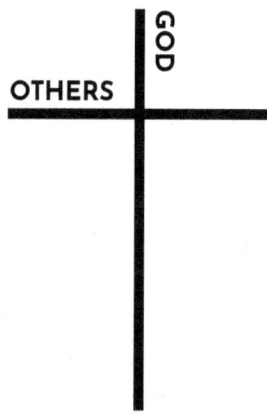

Yes, my friend, that's the cross. Developing both types of relationships gives us the fullness God has for us.

Investing in healthy relationships with God and others is an important part of our physical, emotional, and mental health. Unfortunately, sometimes our relationships with others can get tricky, which is why we'll be discussing boundaries next.

Chapter 5

HOW CAN I SET BOUNDARIES IN MY RELATIONSHIPS?

As a personal trainer, I have to be available when my clients have time to train. If I want to work with teen girls, that means I can't train them at 8:30 a.m. while they are in school.

Because I'm a people pleaser at heart, I try hard to accommodate those I work with. But if I'm not careful, my desire to help them can hurt other relationships that are important to me.

I've had requests for training sessions on Tuesdays at 8 p.m. and on Saturday mornings. Am I available? Technically, yes. However, my evenings are intentionally focused on my family, and Saturday mornings are for my husband, coffee, and lounging in pajamas.

If I don't create boundaries, helping others will hurt me and my closest relationships.

You probably have relationships with various people: friends, teachers, coaches, youth group leaders. Oh yeah, and your parents.

At some point, you may be asked to do something that would make you too busy to function or wouldn't fit into your schedule well—or that, maybe, you just flat-out don't want to do. But if you're a people pleaser like I am, saying "no" makes your stomach clench up.

What might you need to say "no" to? That will vary from person to person. But here are a few areas that may need a boundary:

- » **Overcommitment.** Things like joining student council, volunteering at a local pet shelter, or babysitting are all great on their own. But if they start interfering with other parts of your life, it may be time to back off. You don't need to be everything to everyone.

- » **Unhealthy relationships.** That friend who makes you feel worse about yourself every time you're with her? I'm talking about her. At a minimum, say "no" to confiding in her and see how you can reduce the time you spend with her. If necessary, mute, block, or remove her from your online friend list.

- » **Negative self-talk.** Did you know that your thoughts impact your body as well as your mind? We will dig into this more in an upcoming chapter, but it's important to know that tearing yourself down impacts your health more than you think.

- » **Unsafe situations.** Obviously. If something puts you at risk physically, emotionally, or mentally, it's a hard no. *(See the Pro Tip below if you find yourself in an unsafe situation.)*

- » **Screen time.** Don't worry—I'm not saying you need to log off completely. But if you're losing out on sleep or putting off homework because you're caught in a YouTube binge or losing your day sixty seconds at a time on TikTok, it's time to put the screens away.

Now, there *are* some things you just have to say "yes" to because it's what your family needs, like visiting your elderly Aunt Margaret or doing your chores. But there's a time and a place for respectful conversation about why you'd like to say "no" to something.

Now Say "No"

Once you've identified what to say "no" to, learn how to say it. One kind way is to make a multi-layered sandwich:

» Express appreciation or a positive statement. "Thank you so much for thinking of me…"

» Be direct and honest. "…but I'm unable to come to that party on Saturday…"

» When necessary, use "I" statements. "…because I feel (stressed, overcommitted, not right)…" (Or you can skip this part if you don't feel like explaining!)

» End with alternatives, compromises, or an affirmation. "…but if something changes, I'd love to be involved in a different way."

Pro Tip: *If you are in an unsafe situation, you don't need to use this strategy. Use a firm, assertive "no" to get the point across. You can even raise your voice if you need to. "No" is a complete sentence!*

Let's use an example of when I volunteered at a pet adoption foundation and needed to stop. I told them, "I love these animals and enjoy helping them find new homes, but I can't volunteer here any more. My allergies get so bad that I'm miserable. But when I hear about someone wanting a new dog, I'll refer them to you." The shelter appreciated my honesty, and I physically and mentally felt better about leaving in a clear way.

Saying "no" may be uncomfortable, but it's helpful for you and for others. And often, people are more understanding than you might expect. I've even had people tell me "good for you" when I've had to say "no" to protect my time or mental health.

Recently, I was invited to a going-away party for a friend who was moving. At the same time, my son came home for two weeks in between his summer commitment and college, both of which are in a different state. I reached out to my friend and said, "I'm so sorry to do this, but my son is only home for two weekends before he leaves again. I just want to soak up all the time with him that I can. I hope you have a wonderful time at your party and feel loved and cherished!" Her response? "I don't blame you! Enjoy every moment" (also sent with a bunch of smiling and love emojis). She had a wonderful party, I got time with my kid, and we still cared for each other.

Saying "no" is a practice, both with others and yourself. The more you do it, the more confident you will be. Define and create boundaries so you and your relationships are protected. You are worth it.

Chapter 6

E – WHAT DOES IT MEAN TO TAKE CARE OF MYSELF?

Have you ever been told by a teacher, coach, parent, or other adult to take care of yourself? My guess is yes. My kids heard it from basketball coaches, health teachers, and guest speakers at their school. And they obviously heard this from their mom and dad.

You probably know how important it is to take care of yourself, but have you ever wondered what that even means? It's so vague! It's like telling a track athlete to pass the person in front of them to win the race. Obviously that's what we want, but how do we get fast enough to actually achieve that?

Taking care of yourself is about so much more than what you eat and how you move. It's made up of multiple areas that work together to create a healthy you. I call this holistic health.

Spoiler alert: it's basically *everything*, which is what the E in CORE Strength stands for. **Everything counts in a health journey**, not just food and fitness.

Here are seven areas to consider when taking care of your health:

1. Get at least seven hours of sleep each night.

We will discuss sleep more in Chapter 9, but getting enough quality sleep with as few interruptions as possible (phone notifications, I'm talking about you!) is one of the foundations of health.

2. Drink at least sixty-four ounces of water a day.

Keeping your body hydrated with water is vital to holistic health. It helps regulate your body temperature, transports nutrients where they need to go, and supports digestion. When you're dehydrated, your energy levels and mental alertness go down. And if you exercise recreationally or as an athlete, hydration impacts performance. Aim to drink at least sixty-four ounces a day, or more if you're outside or sweating a lot. Chapter 13 provides tips on drinking more if you have a hard time with that.

3. Eat food.

It's that simple. The food chapters in Part Two go into more detail about different types of food, but before getting too concerned about *what* you eat, make sure you are eating *enough*.

4. Establish and keep boundaries.

As we just discussed, taking care of yourself involves establishing boundaries with your friends, your time, and the words you say to yourself. A clear "no" is helpful to everyone.

5. Move your body.

God designed us to move. We were never meant to spend our days staring at a glass rectangle while lying horizontally on the couch for hours. We'll talk a lot more about exercise later on, but in the meantime, know that it's important to work some kind of movement into most days. Walking, athletics, swimming, dancing, and bike riding are all included.

6. Take care of your mental health.

Have you ever bitten into a shiny, gorgeous apple only to find out that it's bruised and battered on the inside? Walking around with a fake smile and pretending everything is fine when we are hurting on the inside will cause us to look and feel like that bruised apple. We'll talk more about mental health and how to take care of it later.

7. Keep tabs on your emotional health.

Emotional well being involves understanding and managing your emotions, developing healthy coping mechanisms, and creating positive relationships (R in CORE Strength!). It is one part of your mental health that focuses on expressing your emotions in a healthy way. Learning to clearly express what you need is hard, but worth it. Journaling, therapy, and meditation can all help you process your emotions.

> **Pro Tip:** *Sometimes caring for our emotions means having hard conversations. Have something hard to say? Apply the sandwich method. Your positive comments are the bread and the hard comments are the meat in the middle. "I really like spending time with you, but when*

> *you make fun of other people, it makes me worried that you're doing the same thing to me when I'm not around. I really enjoy laughing at puppy reels with you—can we do that instead?"*

Do I have to be perfect at this?

Absolutely, positively not! Some areas of taking care of yourself will be easier than others. Some areas may need more focus at times while others wait in the background. One of my clients had to back off from her athletic training for a while so she could focus on her mental health. I was so proud of her for doing that, even though she wasn't exercising as much.

You may find that one area, like exercising, is easy to do, but choosing foods that make you feel and function well is harder. (Not sure what I mean by "feel and function well?" Stay tuned; we will discuss this more later!) Or you might need to invest time in talking with a mental health professional rather than focusing on exercise and food choices if doing so has become an obsession.

However you feel about these eight areas, keep this truth in mind as we dive deeper into this book:

You do not have to be a straight-A student in the subject of your health.

Heaven knows you already feel enough pressure to make good grades. We don't need to add more to that.

In fact, you aren't being graded at all.

You do not have to be a straight-A student in the subject of your health. In fact, you aren't being graded at all.

Why? Because *you* have to determine what is best for you, now and for your future self. There's no one-size-fits-all scorecard. This isn't a Scantron or multiple-choice exam. This is just me providing science-backed information to help your body, mind, and soul feel nourished. What you do with that information is up to you.

I truly believe that the more you learn about what makes your body feel best, the more you'll choose the foods and movement that support that. Read this book and apply what works for you. Know that *you are in charge of taking care of yourself.* Even picking up this book and thumbing through it is a huge step in doing so. I'm proud of you!

Chapter 7

HOW DO I KNOW IF I'M HEALTHY?

Pretend an alien from outer space was dropped into our American culture and given Instagram. If you typed in #healthy (or pretty much any other variation of that) and asked them to define "health" based on what they saw, how do you think they would respond?

My guess is:

- » Having a lean body with super defined muscles
- » Eating food that makes for pretty pictures
- » Exercising... a lot

This may surprise you, but I'm going to argue that these things don't actually mean someone is healthy. One reason is that we have no idea what these people are doing to look that way. Also, as we know, the picture doesn't share the full story. Skin-perfecting, sparkle-producing, and light-diffusing filters abound. And we tend to only show our good sides on social media. While I pride myself on being real on the socials, I don't exactly put up pictures of my T-shirts that show swoob (sweaty boob) or the acne that still pops up every now and then. So no, what we see isn't fully real. And those pictures don't define health either.

To be clear: health does not have a specific look. But if we can't define health by what we see, how *can* we define it? First, let's talk about what does NOT indicate health:

1. Weight ≠ Health

As we will discuss, weight does not correlate to health. It's possible to be healthy in a bigger body and unhealthy in a smaller body. Gaining or losing five or ten pounds does not necessarily mean you are more or less healthy.

In fact, the right weight for you may be bigger or smaller than what you want. Consider the set point theory, which states that our bodies have a preset weight baseline hardwired into our DNA. According to this theory, our weight and how much it changes from a set point might be limited. Some of us have higher weight set points than others, and our bodies fight to stay within these ranges.[1]

In other words, this means that, according to this theory, your body is going to be healthiest within a certain size range, whether you like it or not. (Because remember, we are original creations, and our diversity represents the body of Christ.)

2. BMI ≠ Health

BMI (short for Body Mass Index) is basically a ratio of your height to your weight. Because it only measures weight, it doesn't take into consideration other factors like muscle mass and hydration. Muscle tissue is more dense than fat, so it takes up less space. If a body has a high concentration of muscle, the BMI has no way of taking that into account and may categorize that body incorrectly. Want proof? Google "professional athletes with a high BMI." Even the American Medical Association has recently acknowledged it's not a useful health tool, so why are we still focused on it?[2] We shouldn't be.

If we can't tell if someone is healthy by looking at them (and we can't), then what *can* we look at? Here are five metrics to know if you are healthy:

1. Blood metrics

Your blood can tell you all sorts of things about your health, like your hormone levels, cholesterol, and metabolic levels (like your blood sugar). If you're not feeling well, go to a doctor. If what you have isn't easily diagnosable, don't be surprised if the first order you receive is to go to the lab for bloodwork.

2. Sleep quality

A bad night's sleep can make us all feel crummy. This is not made up and probably not news to you, but sleeping poorly does more than just make you tired. The Cleveland Clinic shows several ways sleep deprivation affects your health:

- » Fatigue, low energy, and excessive sleepiness (no shock there)
- » Irritability

- » Brain issues that can cause blurred vision, memory lapse, poor reaction time, and drooping eyelids
- » Lowered immune system response, causing you to get sick more easily
- » Higher-than-normal blood sugar levels
- » Impaired learning, poor concentration, and decreased school performance[3]

Do you know you need to sleep more, but have a hard time doing it? We'll cover this in Chapter 9. But if you're consistently not sleeping well, this is a sign that your short-term and long-term health are suffering.

3. Mental health

Let's say you have a friend who is super focused on eating well and exercising. On a superficial level, she looks like she has it all together, but she's cranky and anxious about every bite of food—and, quite frankly, not super fun to be around.

Would you describe this friend as healthy? Maybe the physical metrics are fine, but from a mental health perspective, I'd argue no. All that stress and anxiety affects the body. Symptoms like upset stomach, headaches, extreme fatigue, breathing problems, pounding heart, and more are all examples of what happens to our bodies when we are stressed.[4]

We'll cover ways to optimize our mental health in the next chapter.

4. Menstrual cycle

Assuming you've already begun having periods, are they occurring regularly? Irregularities in your menstrual cycle (or losing it entirely) could indicate several issues.

Formally known as *amenorrhea*, losing your period is often a sign of a health problem. Possible reasons include:

- » Having a very low intake of calories or fat, low body weight, a low percentage of body fat, or emotional stress. This is called hypothalamic amenorrhea, in which the gland that regulates your cycle slows or stops releasing the hormones that control menstruation.
- » Having PCOS (polycystic ovary syndrome), when a woman's body produces more androgens (a type of hormone) than normal.
- » Thyroid problems, which control metabolism and play a role in puberty and menstruation.[5]

Pro Tip: *The reasons above are for educational purposes and are not intended to diagnose a medical issue. If you're concerned, see a doctor!*

Despite the fact that not getting monthly periods is easier and more convenient, not having regular periods typically means there's something going on that needs attention. Again, talk with a trusted healthcare professional if you're worried so they can take necessary action.

5. Functionality

How well do you go about your day? Can you:

- » Take the stairs without getting winded?
- » Crawl under the couch to get your dog's chew toy?
- » Get through school with enough energy for the day?
- » Step into an impromptu game of spikeball?
- » Run around with the kids at the camp where you volunteer?

These are examples of daily functionality. Basically, how do you feel while you're doing your daily tasks? No matter their shape or size, when our bodies don't function well, we fail to fully thrive.

Your body has a holistic way of telling you if you're healthy. One metric does not tell the whole story, and Instagram *certainly* doesn't. We can't assess health by looking at a single metric, and we certainly can't tell if we're healthy simply by our sizes or weights. Whatever size range your body falls in, it has several ways of communicating its overall health with you as long as you know how to listen.

Part Two

WORK OUT

As promised, here's where we will get into the ins and outs of taking care of ourselves.

I'm calling Part Two "Work Out," but there's much more here than exercise-related questions. Here, "Work Out" means all the details. The food, the movement, the puking (or the prevention of), and, yes, pooping. You can certainly skip around if you want, but I hope you make it through all of the chapters at some point.

Many of these chapters have corresponding resources, whether they are fitness-based videos on YouTube or recipes. I've put all of these resources at the back of the book in the Resource Guide, where you can find them all in one place.

Chapter 8

HOW CAN I TAKE CARE OF MY MENTAL HEALTH?

After I released my first book, *Your Worthy Body*, I knew I wanted to write something similar for young women. Several teen girls graciously read through this book in its earliest stages and provided feedback. One theme I saw over and over was "I want to know how to help my mental health."

I can't express how happy I am that we are openly discussing this. It took way too long for society to catch on that mental health is an integral part of our overall health, and many of us unfortunately learned to suppress our emotions to the degree that our mental health suffered.

While I'm not a therapist, I have discovered some hacks to help my own mental health. I, like practically everyone else, have times when I struggle. When I do, these nine tips are part of my strategy:

1. Protect your sleep

In his book *Keep Sharp*, Dr. Sanjay Gupta writes that "sleep is the single most effective thing we can do to reset our brains and bodies, as well as increase a healthy life span."[1] Think of sleep as a *control-alt-delete* for your brain. It also gives your brain a chance to "clean house" and filter out unnecessary information. Who else feels better when their room is clean? I know I do. And your brain feels better when it's had the chance to clean out everything it doesn't need. Besides, it's hard to make rational decisions and respond well to what's happening around you when you're sleep-deprived (at least it is for me).

(Have problems sleeping? Stay tuned for the next chapter.)

2. Get enough fuel from foods

If you're not fully fed, your brain isn't fully optimized. Feed your body breakfast, lunch, dinner, and any other time you are hungry... even if those around you aren't eating.

Once you know you are giving your brain and body enough energy, play around with foods available to you that can make you feel good. Plant-based foods in particular provide nutrients to help support your brain functionality. And I don't just mean vegetables. Fruits, seeds, nuts, beans, and whole grains like oats, rice, and quinoa all qualify as plants. Many of these are high in magnesium, which is also important for your mental health.

Omega-3 fatty acids also assist in regulating your brain and can help with depression. Find omega-3s in fatty fish like salmon or steelhead trout, flaxseeds, walnuts, and chia seeds.

Think of sleep as a control-alt-delete for your brain.

3. Get outdoors

Spending time outdoors and breathing in fresh air can have a significant impact on your mental health. Even a short walk outside can boost serotonin levels that enhance your mood.[2] Additionally, exposure to natural light during the day can help regulate your sleep-wake cycle, leading to improved sleep quality.[3] (See the Pro Tip in Chapter 9 if you live in a northern climate with little sun in the winter.)

> **Pro Tip:** *Need an excuse to get outdoors? Leash up your dog. I have yet to meet a dog who doesn't want to walk. If you don't have a dog of your own, perhaps your neighbor does—and they might appreciate your offer of dog-walking help!*

4. Move regularly

Physical activity releases endorphins, which can lift your mood. Find an exercise routine that suits your preferences, whether it's walking, jogging, yoga, or any other form of physical activity. Ever heard of the "runner's high?" You don't need to run to get that feeling. Just exercise at a moderate level for twenty minutes or more to receive the benefits of those mood-boosting endorphins.[4]

5. Be mindful

Including mindfulness techniques in your daily routine can help manage stress and enhance your mental well-being. Mindfulness meditation, deep breathing exercises, and journaling can help you stay present, reduce anxiety, and cultivate a sense of calm.

One easy (but admittedly strange) way I do this is by taking three slow belly breaths when I use the bathroom. Take advantage of the time you have by yourself, close your eyes, and breathe deeply through your belly by pretending it's a balloon you're filling up.

Deep breaths also help in stressful moments. Whether it's before a big exam, in the middle of a hard conversation, or before an important game, take a couple of deep, slow breaths to calm your nervous system and do a mini reset. Or try the "box method"—breathe in for four counts, hold for four, breathe out for four, and hold for four. Bonus! You'll see in the next chapter that this may also help with your sleep!

6. Connect with others

Surround yourself with supportive friends and family members who uplift and understand you. Engage in activities and hobbies that bring you joy and allow you to connect with others who share similar interests.

As I shared in Chapter 4, I schedule "walk-and-talks" to build my horizontal relationships. I schedule a time to walk with a friend, either in person or on the phone, and we catch up. Sometimes we keep it light and other times we go deep. I've made valued, wonderful friendships with cherished friends on the sidewalks of my neighborhood, and am so grateful for the time I can spend with them.

7. Think about what you're thinking about

It's time to ghost the Inner Mean Girl living in your head (you know the one … she's constantly telling you you're not enough). Why?

Because the more you think about something, the more hard-wired that thought becomes in your brain.

Think about a trail. The more we walk on it, the more defined the trail gets. The same thing is true with our brains. Repeated thoughts and habits deepen the neural pathways in our brains. Letting the Inner Mean Girl spew her hateful nonsense over and over only makes it easier for her to take over your internal narrative.

The apostle Paul may have been on to something when he wrote this to the Philippians two thousand years ago:

> Finally, brothers and sisters, whatever is true, whatever is noble, whatever is right, whatever is pure, whatever is lovely, whatever is admirable—if anything is excellent or praiseworthy—think about such things. **Philippians 4:8**

Need some inspiration for a positive phrase to repeat when the Inner Mean Girl strikes? Try one of these and adjust it to your liking:

- » I'm still learning
- » I'm doing the best I can
- » This won't last forever
- » I am loved

8. Avoid drugs and alcohol

Even if you aren't old enough to legally drink alcohol, chances are you're around it. There's a ton of research on both alcohol and marijuana and how they negatively impact mental health. Both of these things chemically alter your brain and will hurt your mental health now and later (especially marijuana).[5] It may make you happy or chilled out in the moment, but it will harm your brain in the long run. This also goes for your friends' medications, like ADHD drugs. If your name isn't on the medicine bottle, it's not meant for your brain, so don't take it!

Additionally, alcohol and marijuana prevent you from getting deep sleep, which your brain needs for optimal health.[6] While both may help you fall asleep, your sleep quality won't be restorative. I've listed some podcasts that can help you learn more in the Resource Guide.

If you or a friend turns to alcohol, vaping, marijuana, or more to deal with struggles or issues at home, please consider quitting and seeking the help of a therapist instead. If you need help quitting, there are specialists for that as well. This is a healthier way of managing these anxieties and can help you build a strong foundation for coping with the stresses of life now and later.

9. Consider seeing a therapist

You've probably grown up going to a pediatrician for checkups at least once a year. Just like we visit physicians to help our bodies, mental health professionals like therapists and psychiatrists care for our brains. Therapists offer skills that you can't always get from friends or loved ones. They provide a safe and nonjudgmental space to openly express and explore your thoughts, emotions, and challenges.

You don't need to have a problem to visit a therapist, either. I visit mine about once a month for check-ins and to process issues I'm having a hard time sorting through on my own. You can find one by asking trusted friends, searching PsychologyToday.com, or utilizing a service like BetterHelp.com. And just like with all relationships, it's okay if you don't click with the first therapist you try. I once interviewed a therapist who told me it took her three times to connect with the right person. Keep trying!

«»

I'm so grateful we can talk openly about our mental health. Thank you to Simone Biles, Selena Gomez, Mandisa, and other brave women for letting us know that it's okay not to be okay and encouraging us to get the help we need.

These tactics are not the end-all-be-all, but they are a helpful start in promoting good mental health. Remember: it's just as worthwhile to take care of your mind as it is to take care of your body.

Chapter 9

HOW DO I SLEEP BETTER?

One day when I was in high school and looking for an easy way to lose weight, I drove myself to the nearest GNC and bought some weight loss pills. I stuffed them into my backpack, snuck them into my room, and took the recommended two-pill dose after dinner. A few hours later, I lay awake in bed watching the clock tick later and later while the window of time I had left for sleeping got smaller and smaller.

I don't recommend any of this. I plunked down my hard-earned babysitting money to pay for something that kept me awake at night and was completely ineffective. It was also dangerous. Those kinds of "supplements" are not regulated by the FDA, so who knows what was actually in that pill. (Also, if I had to sneak and hide a purchase, that was probably the Holy Spirit nudging me that I shouldn't be doing so.)

Diet pills are generally caffeine in pill form. They just don't work. Once I quit them, my sleep returned to normal.

Maybe you're smarter than I was and you don't take diet pills. Good for you. But there may be other things keeping you awake at night. School, friendships, and family dynamics are enough to keep anyone's mind churning into the wee hours of the morning. But some reasons for insomnia are more controllable than others.

Here are a few tricks to help you get more sleep. I can't guarantee you'll sleep as well as Jesus did in the boat during a storm (check out Matthew 8:23–27 for that full story), but try the **SLEEP WELL** approach. SLEEP focuses more on physical changes while WELL focuses on mindset.

SLEEP

Screens

Ugh, I know. I hate that I started with this too, but it worked well in my acronym, so it stays. My phone is what connects me to my friends and family, but that same phone emits blue light, which can disrupt the body's natural sleep-wake cycle and suppresses the production of melatonin, the hormone that regulates sleep. Try not to use screens at least an hour before bedtime.

Light

Get it at the beginning and end of your day. If possible, get outside shortly after waking up and get ten to fifteen minutes of sunlight... and here's the key... *without* sunglasses. This helps set your circadian rhythm and tells your brain it's officially daytime. In turn, your brain will release melatonin later in the day. For some bonus light therapy, step outside as the sun sets to help your brain know it's almost time for bed.

Pro Tip: *If your weather, climate, or latitude prohibits you from getting early morning sunlight, a nice alternative is a UV-free, high-intensity light. I use the Verilux Happy Light in the winter, but you can search for "UV-free therapy light" to find the right one for you.*

Energy drinks, coffee, and other caffeine

I'm not going to recommend anything I'm not willing to do myself. Since my morning routine includes two cups of coffee, I won't ask you to refrain from caffeine entirely. However, this is one topic I feel fairly strongly about, so please indulge me.

Meeting friends at Starbucks is a fun way to connect, and an iced mocha on a July afternoon is refreshing. However, there are a few important things to note about caffeine:

» Caffeine has a half-life of four hours. Say you meet a friend for a pumpkin spice latte around 4 p.m. A grande size contains about 150 milligrams of caffeine. Four hours later, you still have half of that, or 75 milligrams of caffeine, pumping through your system. Instead, try an iced passion tango tea (caffeine-free) or a refresher (50 mg).

» Energy drinks contain about 200 milligrams of caffeine, or the equivalent of two cups of coffee. They're also full of sugar and/or artificial sweeteners, which means we can chug one in about five minutes if we need to. Funneling 200 milligrams of caffeine into your system in such a short amount of time is hard on your heart, and your system is going to have to work overtime to process all of it. I'm trying hard not to put on my mom hat and plead with you to not use or abuse energy drinks, but my kids will verify that I strongly dislike them.

» Be aware of sneaky sources of caffeine, like chocolate, matcha, kombucha, pre-workout supplements, and pain relievers like Excedrin. And, of course, caffeine is in those diet pills I really hope you don't take. If your doctor has prescribed stimulant medications for migraines or ADHD, talk with them if your sleep is impacted.

» Your body can develop a tolerance to caffeine, meaning that over time, you'll have to ingest bigger and bigger doses to get the same effect.

» There's no proven safe limit for caffeine in children under twelve, and in general, pediatricians advise limiting caffeine to 100 milligrams daily, or one cup of coffee. Choose wisely what you have and when you have it.

» Caffeine has been found to intensify anxiety in those who suffer from anxiety disorders.[1] If you already have anxiety, reducing (or, ideally, eliminating) caffeine intake can help.

Eat foods high in magnesium

Magnesium helps calm the nervous system, regulate stress, support melatonin production, and relax your muscles. Magnesium-rich foods like leafy green vegetables (including broccoli, spinach, and kale), avocados, nuts, seeds, and whole grains can help provide adequate levels of magnesium. My go-to magnesium builder is avocado toast on wheat bread sprinkled with crushed red pepper and drizzled with honey for a sweet kick.

*P*hysical activity

We will discuss movement in more detail later, but in general, ensure that you are moving enough throughout most days. Even a ten-minute leisurely walk (sleep bonus: around sunrise or sunset) can help.

WELL

*W*orry journal

Sometimes just naming what is bothering us can help diffuse anxiety. Keep a pad of paper and a pen by your bed, and when you just can't get something out of your mind, try writing it down. Concerned about privacy? Take that piece of paper, tear it up, and throw it away in the morning. Since we're trying to limit screen usage (see above), don't write it out on your phone.

*E*xecute the box breathing method

Breathe in for four counts, hold your breath for four, slowly exhale for four, and hold again for four. As you exhale, relax your chest, neck, and belly. This specific type of slow breathing can help you fall asleep and lull you back to sleep if you wake up in the middle of the night. It can calm your nervous system, regulate your breathing, and lower the stress hormone cortisol, which can keep you awake.[2]

*L*imit clock watching

Constantly tapping your phone to see what time it is not only adds to your stress, but it's also giving you another shot of blue light, which keeps you up. Resist the temptation to keep track of the time by staring at your phone or even the clock ticking away across the room. It will only stress you out more.

Lay your worries at Jesus' feet

In Matthew 11:28, Jesus invites us to "come to me, all you who are weary and burdened, and I will give you rest." Visualize what is bothering you and then imagine yourself putting it down in front of Jesus. When I find myself awake in the middle of the night (yes, it happens to me too), I've started taking time in the quiet stillness to pray for my friends. I often fall asleep soon after doing this, so I'm not sure if that means I'm a good or bad friend, but it does seem to settle my heart and mind and help me drift back to sleep.

What about melatonin supplements?

Fair question. Melatonin seems to be everywhere right now. Remember, this is a hormone that we naturally produce. The **SLEEP WELL** tactics listed above should help you regulate your melatonin levels without the need for supplements. Please try those first!

Popping a melatonin gummy to make yourself sleepy may seem easier, but is it the best alternative? In my opinion, no, but that's a discussion for you, your parent, and your physician to have. This is a PWC (proceed with caution) supplement, as melatonin overdoses have increased over 420% from 2009 to 2020, mostly among adolescents.[3] Additionally, as mentioned above with those awful "diet pills," supplements are not regulated by the FDA, so it's hard to know if what's listed in the ingredient list is actually in the product. Again, proceed with caution and with the guidance of your parent and/or physician.

But is sleep really that important?

Yes, my friend. Yes it is. You'll hear me discuss sleep often in this book. In fact, I think it's one of the first things we should focus on when taking care of our health. It's *that* important. If you gain nothing else from this book other than taking care of your sleep, you've succeeded. Sleep impacts our mental health, our hormones, our recovery, and more. It is worth creating boundaries and saying "no" to things to get quality sleep.

If you try these **SLEEP WELL** approaches and you're still fighting to get enough zzzz's, reach out to your physician to ensure you don't have underlying medical issues. But take the time to try these tactics. It's not easy, but it's worth the effort.

Chapter 10

WHAT DO YOU MEAN THERE ARE NO "GOOD" AND "BAD" FOODS?

In seventh grade, I got a rare bad grade on an English paper and had to get my mother's signature. I knew I'd get in trouble, so I did something I'd never done and haven't done since: I forged her signature. Even now, decades later, I still feel guilty about doing this.

Forging my mom's signature was inarguably the wrong thing to do. I was anxious for days, hoping my teacher wouldn't figure it out. To my knowledge, she didn't, and Mom, I'm ashamed you're having to find out this way. Please forgive me.

Actions like that have obvious "good" or "bad," "right" or "wrong" choices and outcomes associated with them. But when we start putting labels like "good" and "bad" on food, we internalize those same feelings of guilt, shame, and anxiety. It can also give us a false sense of pride for eating food we think is "right." Either way, we start to associate our self-worth with the food we eat.

For example, we think that when we have a salad we are "good" and that indulging in ice cream is "bad." However, we are still the same person no matter what we eat because food does not have morals. All food gives us energy, whether it's pizza, pickles, or pineapple. In the next few chapters, we will talk more about which foods can help us feel good, but the takeaway here is that you should eat foods because they make you *feel* good, not because you think they *are* good.

Instead of labeling food as "good" or "bad," think about what you eat in a different way.

- » **Listen to your body.** You were born with cues like hunger, fullness, and satisfaction. When you pay attention to those cues and respond, you're more likely to feel nourished and satisfied.

- » **Avoid restricting.** Research indicates that those who severely restrict certain foods or food in general are more likely to experience episodes of binge eating.[1]

- » **Seek satisfaction.** When you eat, whatever you eat, enjoy it. What's the purpose in shoving as many chips and queso in your mouth as quickly as you can if you aren't even going to enjoy it? You don't have taste buds in your stomach. Enjoy your food while you chew it (and for heaven's sake, don't add a heaping side of shame while you do).

You'll frequently hear me advocating for eating nutritionally dense foods (we will cover this more in Chapter 12). This does not mean they are "good" foods. It means that when you feed your body enough (as you should), they are likely to help us feel better in our bodies and minds when we eat them and they will honor our well-being.

There's plenty of science to support eating this way, also called eating *real* foods or *whole* foods (not to be confused with the grocery store). At the same time, there's plenty of science that associates stress with negative effects on the body.[2] It's easy to get stressed about eating the "right" or "good" foods if we label them that way.

So what's a girl to do?

Take the nutrition information you need now and leave the rest for later.

Don't stress about getting it all right. If the only thing you apply right now is that you begin eating enough consistently to fuel your brain and body, that's okay.

If you find yourself getting too hung up on and stressed about what you eat, I recommend checking out *The Intuitive Eating Workbook for Teens: A Non-Diet, Body-Positive Approach to Building a Healthy Relationship with Food* by Elyse Resch. It is a wonderful workbook to help you make peace with food and your body.

God gave us some incredible foods. He gave us even more incredible bodies. Trust your body to know what you need. (Also, trust me: don't forge your parent's signature on a paper. Even if you get away with it, it will eat you up until you're forty-nine years old and you confess to it in a book.)

Chapter 11

WHAT DOES "DIET CULTURE" MEAN?

Do you have any regrets? I sure do. I could tell you about the time I accidentally shamed a classmate in my geometry class for not being on the varsity football team, or the time I made an insensitive and ignorant statement in my Women in Business class in college. I desperately wish I could go back and change some of the things I said.

I also wish I could go back to my younger self and change some of the things I told myself. Things like:

> » "You'll be happier if you're ten pounds thinner."
>
> » "You need to skip breakfast…you had dessert last night."
>
> » "You'd better double it up at the gym today because you missed yesterday's workout."

I now know my thinking was entrenched in diet culture.

Have you heard the term "diet culture?" Honestly, it's not something I was familiar with until I began having conversations about it on my *Graced Health* podcast a few years ago.

There is no official definition for diet culture, though many people define it similarly. In general, diet culture is a set of beliefs and practices that worship thinness and equate body size with health or morality. It is the lens through which beauty is commonly viewed and defined.[1] Additionally, diet culture demonizes certain foods and food groups while elevating others.[2]

Diet culture uses food and exercise as a way to manage our God-given body size, rather than honoring the God-given body we have.

As I have learned (and continue learning) about diet culture, I admit that practically everything I thought was "healthy" has been turned upside down.

A few examples:

OLD THINKING	NEW THINKING
I need to reach my goal weight.	My original body has a natural set point where it will fight to stay.[3] "Goal weights" are arbitrary, man-made numbers.
There are "good" and "bad" foods.	All foods provide energy.
Skipping meals or restricting certain foods will help me lose weight.	Severely restricting foods can result in binge eating.[4] (No wonder I ate the entire pantry at 4 p.m. after undereating during breakfast and lunch!)

OLD THINKING	NEW THINKING
I need to be hyperfocused on what I eat.	Stress, including being stressed about what we eat, is harmful to our health by affecting our sleep and contributing to high blood pressure, depression, and anxiety.[5]
A detox will help clean me out.	My body has a wonderful system to detox on its own through peeing, pooping, and sweating.
If I want to be healthy, I need to eat the "right" foods and exercise.	Health is so much more than food and exercise; it also includes our mental health, relationships, stress levels, and sleep.

If you need to, read those over and take a minute (or an hour) to digest it. I'll be honest: reframing health this way takes time. I'm *still* learning!

But it makes sense: God didn't create us to all look alike. He gave us smart bodies that know when we are hungry and when we are satiated. Just like he made us with different skin tones, eye shapes, and hair color, He also gave us different heights and sizes. As registered dietitian and author Leslie Schilling teaches in her book *Feed Yourself*, body diversity is divine.[6]

> **Pro Tip:** *Read Leslie's book Feed Yourself to learn more about diet culture, divine diversity, and declaring our bodies to be good and wise.*

The diversity God created does not and should not fit into a particular size. He doesn't ask us to do that. Unfortunately, diet culture does.

Remember the goal I mentioned in the Introduction? I aim to provide applicable, sustainable, and truthful nutrition. I believe that ditching diet culture is the way to do that. And those are words I know I will *not* regret saying.

Chapter 12

WHAT FOODS HELP MY BODY FEEL GOOD?

My older son worked incredibly hard to play varsity basketball in high school. In addition to school practices, he also worked with a private coach. One day, when he was coming home from practice, he called me yelling, "Get the gun! Get the gun!"

What? Where are you? What's going on? Also ... a gun? What in the world?

These are just a few of the questions I spewed off in about three seconds.

Turns out, he meant to get a *percussion* gun, which uses vibrations to help get blood flow to aching or cramping muscles and relax them. That made so much more sense! He was in his car in our garage, and on the ride home from practicing with his coach, his muscles cramped up to the point of not being able to move them.

Too bad we didn't have a percussion gun (but we did have a great Christmas idea after that)! Instead, I went into full-on Nutrition Coach mode and got him foods and drinks high in the micronutrients his body needed.

This is just one example of how we can use foods to help our body feel good.

All about nutrients

Merriam-Webster defines "nutrient" as "furnishing nourishment; a substance or ingredient that promotes growth, provides energy, and maintains life."[1] Nutrients as I'm defining them here—as the building blocks of our foods—can be broken down into macronutrients and micronutrients.

You've probably heard of carbohydrates, proteins, and fats, also called macronutrients. But micronutrients are smaller powerhouses within those bigger categories that help our body optimally run. All foods have at least one macronutrient, and within that macronutrient are one or more micronutrients.

Foods that have a high concentration of macro and micronutrients are considered *nutritionally dense*. This is a term I'll use throughout this book.

The chart on the next page shows how micronutrients can be tied to more than one macronutrient.

While macronutrients and micronutrients don't sound very exciting, understanding them can help your body and brain feel good.

Let's look at them individually.

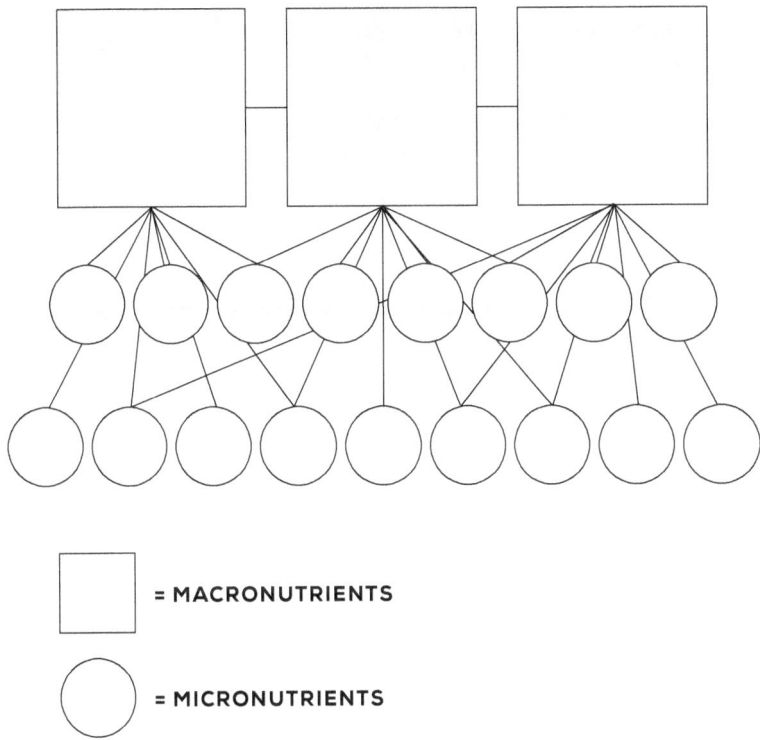

Macronutrients

All foods contain at least one of three macronutrients: carbohydrates, proteins, and fats. And we need all of the macronutrients! Some foods, like chicken breasts, may have mostly protein, little fat, and no carbohydrates. Other foods, like strawberries and rice, are mostly carbohydrates. And nuts, which are one of my favorite foods, are mostly protein and fat.

Here's a little more on how each macronutrient benefits our body:

MACRONUTRIENT	ROLE	FOUND IN
Carbohydrates (see Chapter 17)	Provide energy to your muscles and brain; includes fiber (see Chapter 29)	Fruit, some vegetables, and grains
Protein (see Chapter 15)	Makes muscles and tissues; plays a role in carrying oxygen throughout the body; repairs muscles damaged from working out; helps protect your immune system	Meat, fish, eggs, dairy, beans, legumes
Fats (see Chapter 16)	Help your body absorb certain vitamins; help you feel satisfied when you eat; give you energy	Monounsaturated fats found in olives, nuts, seeds, and fatty fish; other fats found in animal-based products; fried foods

You need all three of these macronutrients to thrive.

Want proof? Look at the foods God provided in the garden of Eden. We can't get out of the first book of the Bible without witnessing God's provision: "I give you every seed-bearing plant on the face of the whole earth and every tree that has fruit with seed in it. They will be yours for food" (Gen. 1:29). Later, He includes animals: "Everything that lives and moves about will be food for you. Just as I gave you the green plants, I now give you everything" (Gen. 9:3).

I know there's a lot of noise about carbs, proteins, and fats, and it seems that "diet rules" are always changing (which is one of many reasons we need to ditch diet culture). We'll cover each of these macronutrients more in upcoming chapters.

Micronutrients

Micronutrients are vitamins and minerals that are all needed in the body, but in smaller amounts. They are small but mighty and can make a world of difference in how we feel and function.

Micronutrients remind me of all of the roles necessary to make a production succeed. I recently went to see the singer P!nk in concert. While she was the one singing, there were countless people in the background supporting the performance. The sound, lighting, and prop technicians—and even her acrobatic trainer—all contributed. There's no way that concert would have been as mighty as it was without all of those unseen roles.

The point is, micronutrients do a lot of work in the background that impacts how our bodies and brains feel. That's why you'll hear me refer to them as the Mighty Micronutrients.

Vitamins:

VITAMIN	ROLE	FOUND IN
A	Supports vision, immune function, and cell growth	Carrots, sweet potatoes, spinach, kale, mangoes, apricots
D	Promotes calcium absorption for healthy bones and teeth, plays a role in immune function, may help reduce inflammation, and regulates hormones	Fatty fish (salmon, mackerel, sardines); cod liver oil (ew, but okay); fortified dairy products (milk, yogurt, cheese); fortified cereals; egg yolks; sunshine
E	Acts as an antioxidant, protecting cells from damage; supports immune function	Almonds, sunflower seeds, spinach, avocado, olive oil, wheat germ
K	Essential for blood clotting and bone health	Leafy greens (kale, spinach, broccoli, Brussels sprouts); green peas; parsley; cabbage
B vitamins: B1 (thiamine), B2 (riboflavin), B3 (niacin), B6 (pyridoxine), B12 (cobalamin folate)	Necessary for energy production, red blood cell formation, and nervous system function	Whole grains (oats, brown rice, quinoa); legumes (beans, lentils); meat (poultry, fish, beef); dairy products; leafy greens
C	Supports immune function and collagen synthesis; acts as an antioxidant	Citrus fruits (oranges, lemons, grapefruits); strawberries; kiwis; bell peppers; broccoli; tomatoes

Minerals:

MINERAL	ROLE	FOUND IN
Calcium*	Essential for bone and dental health, muscle function, and nerve transmission	Dairy products (milk, cheese, yogurt); leafy greens (kale, spinach, collard greens); fortified plant-based milk (soy milk, coconut milk, almond milk); tofu; sardines (with bones)
Zinc	Plays a role in immune function, wound healing, and growth and development	Shellfish (oysters, crab, mussels); beef; pumpkin seeds; chickpeas; yogurt; cashews
Magnesium*	Involved in hundreds of body systems, including energy production, muscle and nerve function, and bone health	Nuts (almonds, cashews); seeds (pumpkin seeds, flax seeds); leafy greens; avocados; legumes (black beans, lentils); whole grains (brown rice, whole wheat, quinoa)
Potassium*	Supports proper fluid balance, nerve function, and muscle contraction	Bananas; oranges; spinach; sweet potatoes; avocados; white beans
Sodium*	Required for fluid balance, nerve transmission, and muscle function	Table salt; broth; soy sauce (note: in general, we get more than enough sodium in our diets, so you don't need to be intentional about adding it to your diet unless you're exercising heavily outdoors)

---

* Calcium, magnesium, potassium, and sodium are all electrolytes, which help balance your fluids. If your urine is clear but you have a headache and you've exercised recently, it may be that your electrolytes are off or you haven't eaten enough to refuel. Try consuming foods in these categories and see if that helps.

MINERAL	ROLE	FOUND IN
Iron	Required for the production of red blood cells and oxygen transport	Red meat (beef, bison, lamb); spinach; legumes (lentils, chickpeas); fortified cereals; pumpkin seeds; quinoa

> **Pro Tip:** *If there are new or different foods you'd like to try after reading this list, make a list and give it to the person who does the shopping at your house. Ask them, "Next time you go to the store, can we get these so I can try them?" Then—and this is important—actually try the food you request. Bonus points if you go to the store with the shopper and help!*

As you can see, many foods offer a variety of micronutrients. This is one reason you'll hear me talk so often about the benefit of eating a variety of plants. You don't need to have all of them every day, but eating lots of plants in general will likely give you what you need to be healthy and thrive.

What do I need?

Are there any particular micronutrients you need as your body is still maturing? I'm so glad you asked! These are the four I recommend being intentional about including in your diet:

» **Calcium.** Every time I take my kids to the pediatrician, the physician asks if they are drinking milk. That's because milk is a wonderful source of calcium, which helps your bones develop. Here's the thing: your bones grow stronger until you're about twenty-six, which is called "peak bone mass." After that, they won't get stronger. Get your calcium now while your bones are still developing. Don't like regular milk? Try chocolate milk. It's also a great post-workout snack!

» **Iron.** If you have heavy menstrual periods, you may be losing a lot of iron. Iron-rich foods like red meat, spinach, and dark beans can help resupply your iron after your menstrual cycle.

Almost 40% of American teenage girls and young women have low levels of iron, and nearly 1 in 4 are iron deficient.[2] Symptoms of iron deficiency in young women can be subtle and are often overlooked, including fatigue, cold hands and feet, hair loss, brittle nails, and cognitive issues like brain fog.[3] If you're experiencing these symptoms, chat with your doctor and see if they want you to increase your intake of iron-rich foods.

» **Vitamin D.** Fun fact: vitamin D is actually a hormone that we classify as a vitamin. It has so many benefits, as listed in the table above. The best part about vitamin D? You can step outside and get some. (Don't live in a sunny climate? Ask your physician if a vitamin D supplement is right for you.) The sun provides the best source of vitamin D, but we spend so much time indoors and wear sunscreen outside that we don't get enough. Put some sunscreen on your face only and get outside for fifteen to twenty minutes a day if possible. If you're highly prone to sunburn or at elevated risk of melanoma, ask your dermatologist or dietitian how they recommend you getting vitamin D without harming your skin.

» **Magnesium.** There isn't enough space in this entire book to talk about all the ways magnesium helps our bodies. It might be my favorite micronutrient! You'll see it listed in this book as helping your sleep and mental health, but it also helps your muscles relax. If you get a charley horse (a painful cramp anywhere, but often in the hamstrings or calves) like my son got after basketball, magnesium can help.

We truly do have the power to help our bodies and brains feel well. Use this chapter as a cheat sheet when something doesn't feel right, and see if it helps to add in specific nutritionally dense foods to your day. If you don't feel like anything is improving, it may be worth a visit to your physician or even your mental health provider. You deserve to feel good!

Chapter 13

HOW DO I NOURISH MYSELF?

Think back to the last time you sat around a table with a group and friends and really laughed. You had genuine conversations and felt safe and heard. When it was over, you may have even thought, *wow, I really needed that.*

Now think about what was *on* the table. If one of my sons was answering that question, he'd probably say it was Whataburger with a chocolate shake. The other one may say the Rooty Tooty Fresh 'N Fruity from IHOP. Maybe your example takes place at Starbucks or Chick-fil-A. Mine is at a small-plate restaurant where I've gotten to sample several different foods at once.

Do any of these sound like a perfect balance of nutrients? Not necessarily, and that's okay. But are they nourishing? I say they are.

Dictionary.com defines "nourish" as "to sustain with food or nutriment; supply with what is necessary for life, health, and growth."[1]

Nourishing yourself is much more than choosing the right blend of macronutrients and micronutrients from the last chapter. It's also about surrounding ourselves with the people we care about and filling our souls through laughter, vulnerable conversations, and even tears.

Yes, food is fuel. Food can make the difference between a good and bad workout, how we feel in that after-lunch lull, and even how we sleep. God gave us food to fuel our bodies. He provided plants with many colors and a variety of animals from which to choose. He designed our bodies to need replenishment often. I get to choose from an assortment of foods and eat them several times a day! How glorious is that?

And we now have science sharing how certain nutrients help us feel better. As we talked about in the last chapter, vitamin D can help increase immunity; iron helps transport oxygen; and, of course, basic H_2O supports our entire body.

We've been given so much information about the benefits of the foods we eat that we can forget to acknowledge one of its main benefits: fellowship.

As a Jesus follower, I pay particular attention to how He interacted with others in the gospels. One thing that stands out to me is the many times Jesus spent with His friends while eating. I like to imagine that they laughed and shared stories like we do. Being a bunch of guys, perhaps they even gave each other a hard time. Jesus and His friends spent plenty of time in fellowship around the table, and I'm pretty sure they weren't counting calories or obsessed about how much protein they were getting. They simply enjoyed each other and grew in their friendship.

"Nourishment" is a multidimensional word. Sometimes it's purely the nutrients within the food that promote life, health, and growth. Salads with a variety of colorful toppings certainly fall into this category. Other times, nourishment encapsulates a whole dining experience. It spreads beyond the food we eat and into our very souls.

Life, growth, and health are about more than nutrients. They're made up of experiences. Laughter. Stories. Memories. Bonding.

Of course, there's another kind of nourishment; one that is filled not by foods and relationships but by He who provides us food and relationships: Jesus. I may not fully understand scripture, but I do know that even if every piece of my physical health is perfectly executed, I do not feel complete without Jesus. My morning time with Him in God's Word is critical for establishing my day's foundation.

God nourishes our bodies in so many ways. Sometimes it's through the foods He's given us. Sometimes it's through our relationships and Starbucks runs. But they all provide life, health, and growth. Additionally, He designed our souls to be nourished by Him alone, which also provides life, health, and growth. And that, my friend, is true nourishment.

There's another kind of nourishment; one that is filled not by foods and relationships but by He who provides us food and relationships: Jesus.

Chapter 14

HOW CAN I DRINK MORE WATER?

Each year when I dropped my kids off at summer camp, they had to pass a swim test. This ensured that they could safely enjoy all the activities scheduled for them throughout the week. It was a basic skill set they needed to have, and even the high school seniors had to do it.

We will talk plenty about water in the rest of this book. Consider water like a basic swim evaluation. If you're not drinking enough, nothing else is going to work like you want it to.

Fun fact: About 60% of your body is water, and you lose about twelve cups of water a day in your breathing, talking, digestion, and general activity.[1] Exercising and sweat causes even more loss.

Here are just a few of the ways our body uses water:

- » You know those Mighty Micronutrients we talked about in Chapter 12? You need water to transport them throughout your body.

- » Water helps break down food and takes the nutrients through the intestine wall into the bloodstream.

- » Water eliminates waste products (that's the formal way of saying it, but my way is "water helps you pee and poop").

- » Water maintains healthy skin by providing moisture and promoting a healthy complexion. Want that dewy look? You can't get it if your skin is dehydrated. After all, dew is droplets of water.

- » Water regulates your body temperature.

What if I don't like plain water?

You're not alone. I'm also aware that many people have a hard time drinking enough water. I have people in my life who have this problem too, and we've developed a few hacks to help them drink more.

- » **Experiment with finding what you like to drink from.** A plain glass, a stainless steel mug with a drinkable lid, a wide mouth bottle, or a bottle with a straw are all good options. As strange as it sounds, you may find it easier to drink from one container over another.

- » **Add a squeeze of lemon, orange, or lime.**

Pro Tip: *Cut up one of these citrus fruits and store it in an airtight container in the fridge. It will be ready whenever you want it!*

» Drink caffeine-free herbal tea.

Pro Tip: *You can make this ahead of time and store it in a Mason jar in the refrigerator. There's no rule saying you have to drink hot tea. It can be chilled as well.*

» **Drink sparkling water.** Studies have shown that it's just as hydrating as water.[2]

Pro Tip: *Consuming too many carbonated beverages can make you gassy, so I don't recommend having all sixty-four ounces in your daily recommended allowance this way—that's five whole cans! Stick to one or two cans per day until you know how your body reacts to the carbonation.*

» **Set a timer periodically throughout the day to remind you to drink.**
» **Take several swigs in between periods at school.**
» **Drink an eight-ounce glass of water with breakfast, with lunch, after school, and with dinner.** This gets you halfway to your goal.

Pro Tip: *Drink your water regularly throughout the day and finish around dinnertime so you're not playing catch-up at the end of the day and peeing all night.*

How do you know if you're drinking enough water?

Pay attention to your urine. The darker it is, the more dehydrated you are. Aim for lemonade-colored or lighter urine.

Water, like the math example I used in Chapter 1, is one of our basic, 1+1 foundations of taking care of ourselves. It may take a conscious effort to remember to drink more, but try some of these tricks to help you get enough. Everything else in your health journey will come more easily if you're hydrated enough!

Chapter 15

HOW MUCH PROTEIN DO I NEED?

I was a fairly picky eater growing up. I don't really know or remember why, but I remember gagging on meatloaf night and poking around the casseroles my mom would set in front of us at dinner. Mom always tried to provide nourishing meals in all ways, but that didn't mean I loved it all. God bless her, she rarely showed her frustration, even though I'm sure she felt it. She often responded by telling me to pick out the protein and eat that.

We briefly discussed protein in Chapter 12, but here's a longer list of what protein does:

- » Helps grow muscles, both as your body matures and also after a workout
- » Maintains a healthy metabolism
- » Produces antibodies to support your immune system so you don't get sick as often
- » Repairs damaged tissues (that soreness from a hard workout

is from microtears in your muscles that are damaged and need rebuilding using the protein you consume)[1]

How much protein should I have?

Honestly, that's a tough question to answer because it depends on your activity level and other factors unique to you. Everyone needs protein, but everyone's individual needs vary. I recommend working with a registered dietitian if you have specific questions or needs regarding your protein intake.

Here's a trick: each meal, try to have one serving of protein. Ideally, try to consume around twenty grams with each meal.[2] Your body needs several helpings of protein spread out throughout the day to utilize it best.

Wondering what twenty grams of protein looks like? Here are some options that have around twenty grams of protein *(total approximate grams of protein provided)*:

- » One chicken breast the size of the palm of your hand or a deck of cards (30 g)
- » Two chicken thighs (20 g)
- » Four chicken wings (24 g)
- » 4-oz hamburger patty (28 g)
- » 6.4-oz tuna fish packet (36 g)
- » 2-oz beef stick (23 g)
- » Three hard-boiled eggs (18 g)

- » 1 cup Greek yogurt (about 24 g, but this varies—check the label)
- » 1½ cup extra-firm tofu (30 g)
- » 1 cup beans (any kind) (14–20 g)

Can I have protein powder?

I get this question a lot. In general, I think it's best for growing bodies to get protein in its more natural states. That said, I have protein powder in my pantry for everyone in my house, including my growing boys.

If you choose to use protein powder, I highly recommend getting one that is third-party tested. Protein powder is considered a food *supplement* and is not regulated by the FDA (Food & Drug Administration). For that reason, you don't know if what they say on the label is actually true of what's in the food. NSF and USP are the two dominant third-party testers and will put their logo on the label if it's been tested.

> **Pro Tip:** *Search NSFSport.com for products that they have third-party tested.*

When should I have protein?

In general, get some at each meal, as I mentioned above. Having adequate protein throughout your day will help your muscles rebuild faster, meaning less soreness for you and better performance the next time you exercise.[3]

> **Pro Tip:** *Research shows that you can encourage muscle growth and repair by having twenty grams of whey-based protein at bedtime.*[4] *Whey is the protein found in milk, so you can get this in Greek yogurt, string cheese, cottage cheese, and, of course, milk.*

If you ask a parent of three kids which one is their favorite, they'll say they love all of their kids the same, but they all have unique personalities. The same is true of our macronutrients. Protein is important for everyone regardless of activity level, but fats and carbohydrates are just as important. Read on to learn more!

Chapter 16

WHAT'S THE DEAL WITH FATS?

I recently read a novel set in the 1880s where the doctor used leeches as part of his medical practice. Leeches. Slimy creatures that suck the blood out of you. And this was standard practice. Ew.

Thank the good Lord medicine has evolved.

Nutrition has too. The more we learn, the more we know. But sometimes in the midst of learning, we make mistakes.

The fat-free craze was one of those.

In the 1990s, some researchers proclaimed that dietary fat (fat in our foods) was bad for our heart health, so food companies took out fat and replaced it with sugar.

We now know that this was a terrible, horrible, no-good, very bad idea. Dietary fat is essential for our bodies and brains.

But as a result of the anti-fat craze, there's now confusion about "good" and "bad" fats. What's the deal with that? (Please note I use "good" and "bad" in quotation marks because that's how we often hear about them, not because I agree with assigning moral values to our food.)

Are there different types of fats?

Yes, and they have different effects on the body.

TYPE	ROLE	FOUND IN
Monounsaturated	Promotes a healthy heart by removing LDL (harmful) cholesterol	Olive oil; avocados; nuts; seeds
Polyunsaturated	Helps brain function, mental health, and heart health; reduces inflammation	Plant-based oils like safflower oils; fatty fish like salmon
Saturated	Raises your LDL (harmful) cholesterol, which can increase your risk of heart disease and stroke (not applicable to foods like whole-fat dairy, dark chocolate, and unprocessed meat)[1]	Animal-based meat; fatty cuts of meats
Trans	None	Oily fast foods; certain fried foods (as of 2018, these are not used as much due to an FDA ruling)[2]

Why do I need fat?

Foods like olives, avocados, fatty fish, nuts, and seeds offer wonderful benefits to our bodies, including:

- Being a sustaining energy source (dietary fat provides longer satiety levels, which keep you from feeling hungry after a meal)
- Helping absorb nutrients, especially vitamins A, K, E, and D
- Helping produce various hormones that regulate metabolism, growth, reproduction, and stress
- Supporting mental health by improving mood, memory, and overall brain health and cognition
- Supporting heart health
- Keeping your skin moisturized and increasing skin's elasticity

Just like with proteins, it's a good idea to have a little beneficial fat with your meals. Easy grab-and-go healthy fats include nuts, nut butter, and yogurt.

Is there any time I shouldn't have fat?

The only time I don't recommend having a lot of fat is right before a workout or strenuous activity. Fat takes longer to digest, so it can cause belly discomfort during exercise. Unfortunately, if you're an athlete, the concession stands at your games aren't helpful. Nachos, hot dogs, and chips are all high in fats that won't help your performance (and may make a comeback later via icky burps or vomiting). Instead, opt for pretzels, chips without the nacho sauce, or granola-type bars. Or, if possible, pack a few things from home that will make you…wait for it…feel and function well.

Just like medicine has changed over the years, you'll probably see nutrition recommendations change as you go through life. But I feel pretty solid about this guidance: eat all the foods God gave us…even fats. They are there for a reason.

Chapter 17

ARE CARBS BAD FOR ME?

When I was in high school, we were allowed to go off campus for lunch. My friends and I would speed-walk to Braum's, an ice cream and dairy store that also served burgers and some of the best crinkle-cut french fries you've ever tasted.

I had a budget for lunch, but I also knew if I ordered wisely, I could stretch that money. Day after day, I predictably ordered a peach ice cream cone and a small order of french fries, pocketed the extra money, and picked up some Twizzlers after school.

Just as predictably, I nodded off in fifth-period history *every single day*. You know how your head nods while your eyes roll back and your eyelids feel like they have weights on them? Your brain says STAY AWAKE and the rest of your body screams I NEED SLEEP? Yep, that was me. Every. Day.

Why? Because I loaded my body up on tons of carbohydrates without also giving it the balance of protein.

Does that mean my carb-o-licious meal was bad for me? No, because again, I don't believe there are "good" and "bad" foods.

But was it *good* for me? It didn't help me feel and function well (especially in history class), so I don't think it was the best option for me.

Chances are, you've heard lots of comments about carbs. Some people say they are bad for you or will make you gain weight, but both of those things are untrue. Let's explore this more.

Are carbs good or bad for me?

In my twenty years as a fitness professional, the value of carbohydrates is one of the things I'm asked about the most often.

Let me be crystal-clear in my answer: *carbs are good for you.*

I'll circle back to this in a minute, but first let's get into what carbs do and the confusion we see around carbs.

What do carbs do?

Carbohydrates provide energy to the body and brain. They are made up of various combinations of sugars, starches, and fiber.

Think of them as fuel for all your organs, muscles, and tissues. Your body digests them into glucose and then takes that glucose to several areas:

» **Brain**

Your brain uses about twenty percent of the energy you

Carbs are good for you.

produce from carbohydrates.[1] That headache or brain fog you're experiencing in first period may be from not getting enough beneficial carbs with your breakfast.

» **Bloodstream**

Your blood always holds on to a small amount of glucose in the event that you need a short, quick burst of energy for a few seconds (think: racing upstairs because you forgot your backpack).[2]

» **Liver**

The liver stores a limited amount of glucose to help keep your blood sugar stable in between meals.[3]

» **Muscles**

Your muscles store glucose to be used for exercise and athletics. But in order to have that stored energy, you need to ensure you are fueling up enough prior to the event. Also, if you find yourself in extra long games, try to refuel with some easily digestible foods like simple carbohydrates (see below).

Is there a difference in carbs?

All carbs provide energy to the body. Some carbs provide additional benefits beyond energy.

Remember those nutritionally dense foods listed in Chapter 12? Foods like peaches, potatoes, popcorn, pears, and pinto beans are all nutritionally dense carbs thanks to their Mighty Micronutrients. These provide nutrients and fiber to your body in addition to energy.

Carbs are digested at different rates depending on their structural complexity. Some carbs are slower energy foods, meaning your body takes longer to digest them (thanks to the fiber) and then absorb them into your bloodstream. These are *complex carbohydrates*. They have several energy units strung together in long, complex chains (hence their name).[4] Complex carbs include beans, whole grains, fruits, and nuts.

Other carbs, like Goldfish crackers, Skittles, and pasta provide quick energy. They often have less fiber and fewer nutrients, and your body can quickly uptake them and send them to your blood, brain, liver, and muscles. These are *simple carbohydrates* and were the basis of my high school lunch mentioned above.

Fruit also contains simple carbohydrates. As we've discussed, fruits contain those Mighty Micronutrients that can promote overall wellness. When you eat easily digestible fruits like watermelon, grapes, and bananas, you offer your body fiber, water, and tons of nutrients.

Eating a variety of carbohydrates gives you the full spectrum of value they provide, whether it's being digested more slowly or it's a quick-energy release before an athletic event. As you can see, this isn't a simple-versus-complex carbohydrate issue where one is "bad" and the other is "good." They are just different and have different purposes.

A few years ago, I went camping with a dear friend of mine. My friend is a Scoutmaster with BSA (she leads a troop full of females…how cool is that?) and has extensive knowledge of all things camping. One of the first things we did when we set up camp was start a fire.

After we got the fire going, I noticed how different things we added as fuel burned at different rates. Twigs and leaves would catch fire easily but also burn out quickly. (Yes, conceptually I already knew this, but it was interesting to see.) Larger logs would take a bit to catch fire, but once they did, they would last a while.

Twigs and leaves are like simple carbohydrates. Our body can quickly break them down and utilize the energy they provide. This is why having a snack with some simple carbohydrates before a practice or game can be helpful to give you a quick burst of energy to perform your best.

Logs and hardwood, on the other hand, are like complex carbohydrates. They take longer to burn and provide a steady, sustained release of energy over time.

If carbs are good for me, why do people say they aren't?

Diet culture has assigned moral values with carbs because some are more nutritionally dense than others. For some reason, when people say "carbs," they often mean simple carbohydrates that have fewer nutrients and less fiber. Foods like white bread and pasta get villainized as a "bad carb," but they still provide energy. Labeling all carbs as bad, quite honestly, is uninformed. Carbs can also be found in fruit, grains, nuts, legumes, seeds, dairy products, and sugary foods and sweets. Carbs are everywhere, and for good reason: we need them!

As for bread and pasta, they can be great conduits for having other nutritionally dense foods. You need bread to make a PB&J or turkey sandwich. Spaghetti and meat sauce without the pasta is just meat sauce… that's pretty boring to me. I've been grateful to individual frozen dinner rolls for adding some extra food to my boys' plates. When they were running multiple miles a day or practicing basketball for two hours, those sourdough rolls were a nice addition to the pork chops, asparagus, and sweet potatoes on their plate!

Will carbs make me gain weight?

No. But simple carbohydrates can be easier to quickly consume if we aren't mindful about what we are eating. It's super easy to zone out with a box of crackers while scrolling through the latest Reels in your feed. Before you know it, you've eaten more than you need.

Last night I made taco meat with a mix of beef and lentils served over a baked potato (and of course, I added fixings like cheese, salsa, and avocado!). Even though the potato was small, I didn't finish the entire thing because I was satisfied thanks to the fiber and starch.

It's possible that had I put that same amount of taco meat over potato chips, I would have been able to eat a lot more than my body needed. The potato chips lack the fiber, starch, and general bulk the potato offers.

Want another example? Grab a regular bag of fruit snacks and eat them. Now open a pint of strawberries. These foods have the same amount of energy, but because of the water and fiber in the strawberries, they often take longer to eat.

Potato chips, fruit snacks, and other simple carbohydrates will not make you gain weight. When you do eat them, savor what you eat and stop when you feel satisfied. This will prevent you from eating more than your body needs, which is true for all foods.

Enjoy your carbs

Overall, I think we fail to appreciate all that God has given us when we swear off nutritional building blocks like fats or carbs. Have you ever considered what our biblical ancestors consumed? Check out Deuteronomy 8:7–8:

> For the LORD your God is bringing you into a good land—a land with brooks, streams, and deep springs gushing out into the valleys and hills; a land with wheat and barley, vines and fig trees, pomegranates, olive oil and honey.

Wheat, barley, figs, pomegranates, olive oil, and honey. Sounds delicious! Except for the olive oil, all of these foods contain carbohydrates.

Obviously, there are some medical conditions like diabetes that mean we need different approaches to enjoying carbs, but for the rest of us, it's time we stop thinking of carbohydrates as "good" or "bad" for us and start thinking of them as resources for our body.

In hindsight, I wish I'd understood how my lunch choices affected how I felt back in high school. If I were to make an easy change, I'd swap either the ice cream or fries for a burger, chicken tenders, or a chicken sandwich. Who knows? Maybe that would have kept me awake enough to feel mentally and physically strong and earn an A in the class rather than a B! But there's still time for you—eat the foods God gave us, get out there, and conquer the world (or at least your history class)!

Chapter 18

IS SUGAR BAD FOR ME?

When my boys were younger, I read to them most nights. I admit, reading *Goodnight Moon* approximately three million times got old. As they aged, I delighted in moving to simple chapter books like Junie B. Jones.

I never got tired of Junie B. Jones. This hysterical first-grader called it like she saw it, whether it was appropriate or not. Sometimes I couldn't get through the paragraph because I was laughing so hard.

My friends had kids around the same age as my kids, so I recommended the Junie B. Jones books to them. Later, though, one of my friends texted me, horrified.

"Amy! I can't believe you said this was a good series! Thanks to Junie, my kids now want to put sugar on their strawberries. Sugar is *so bad* for them."

Oops. I hate to disappoint a friend. Also, I hadn't remembered that part.

But was she right? Is sugar bad for them?

There's a lot of confusion out there about sugar. That's understandable. Is it good? Is it bad? Is some okay? What's not okay?

We've already talked about this, but it's worth saying again: My philosophy is there are no "good" and "bad" foods, but there are foods that offer more nutritional value than others.

What does my body do with sugar?

Sugar in any form, whether it's a white cube or amber honey, is quickly digested and pushed into the bloodstream. Because it's a carbohydrate, it's used for energy, like we discussed in the last chapter.

Your body treats all sugar the same way regardless of how it came in. As a simple carbohydrate, it's quickly absorbed into the bloodstream. As your blood sugar rises, your body releases insulin. Insulin regulates the sugar in your bloodstream and takes it to your muscles and liver for energy or to store for future use.[1]

Strawberry Skittles and fresh strawberries both have sugar. Strawberries are more nutritionally dense, carrying beneficial micronutrients like vitamin C, folate, and potassium. Strawberry Skittles, conversely, have fewer micronutrients but sure are delicious and fun to share with a friend. Which one will help us feel and function better? That's for you and your body to decide.

I don't believe every single food we consume needs to have quality nutrients, but it is helpful to have them as part of what you eat in a day. Fresh oranges contain vitamin C, vitamin A, and potassium.

Orange slice candy doesn't have any of these micronutrients but makes for easy, quick energy before practice. What comes along with sugar can make a difference in how everything else functions now and later. We talked about foods that make us feel and function well in Chapter 12. All those micronutrients found in fresh (and frozen) fruit are beneficial, even if there is natural sugar in the fruit.

What is added sugar?

The American Heart Association recommends limiting added sugar to six added teaspoons per day.[2] Added sugar is just that: sugar that is added to food, rather than sugar that occurs naturally in food. You can tell how much added sugar is in the item by looking at the nutrition label. If it's a fresh food, like bananas or watermelon, it doesn't have added sugar.

What is equivalent to six teaspoons of added sugar? There are four grams of sugar in one teaspoon of sugar, so six teaspoons is equal to 24 grams. That is equivalent to a mini 7.5-ounce can of soda, a 3.5-ounce box of Sour Patch Kids, or two regular-sized Reese's peanut butter cups. Some foods have more sugar than you may realize. If you meet a friend at Starbucks and you order a grande java chip frappuccino, you'll consume 59 grams of sugar.

Does that mean I'm saying you shouldn't enjoy that frap with your friends? No. But I believe it's helpful to know so you can make choices that make your body feel good. There are days we all go over this limit, and that's okay.

Keep in mind that the American Heart Association recommendation doesn't allow for our individual needs and nuances. The rate at which your body burns added sugars—and all energy—differs based on your activity level. That's why it's important to take note of how you feel after enjoying a frap or any other meal (see the "Should I avoid sugar" section below).

How do I know if something has added sugar?

Food labels are required by US law to list added sugar, so turn the product around and look at the fine print. Fresh foods like fruits and vegetables are not required to have a food label because there is only one ingredient (and therefore no added sugars). If it's not listed, you can always do some research online. Most companies share nutritional information on their websites, which is how I got my Starbucks numbers for this chapter.

> **Pro Tip:** *If worrying about these numbers causes you stress and results in you not feeding your body enough, skip the label reading all together. It's more important to trust your body than rely on a food label. A fed body is our primary goal; then we can gently incorporate some of these nutritional lessons.*

Why should I care about sugar?

» It offers **little nutritional value** other than quick energy.

» It temporarily **decreases hunger** for other food. Because it is quickly absorbed into your bloodstream, your blood sugar will tell your brain "okay, we're good now," but you still haven't had any of those Mighty Micronutrients, which help our bodies thrive.

» It can **increase the risk of cavities.**

What foods have a lot of sugar that I may not be aware of?

When I was growing up, my church would have cubes of sugar out by the coffee pot. My friends and I would sneak over and grab a cube (or two) after church. Clearly, this is sugar, but sometimes sugar can hide in much less obvious places, like:

» Energy drinks (along with excessive amounts of caffeine, as we discussed in Chapter 9)

» Sodas and coffee beverages

» Granola bars (check the label, as these vary)

» Flavored yogurt

» Condiments and salad dressings

» Fruit juices and other "fruit" drinks

Should I avoid sugar?

Please do not avoid fruits because they have sugar in them! Fruits offer so much other nutritional value. Enjoy however much you want, and just like any other food, stop when you're satisfied.

As for added sugar, that's for you to decide. I recommend paying attention to your added sugar intake and *honestly* assess how you feel. Questions to ask yourself include:

- » Do I feel sleepy or groggy?
- » Do I have brain fog?
- » Is my mental health suffering?
- » Am I sleeping poorly?

If you answered "yes" to any of those questions, experiment with backing off of added sugar intake and see how you feel.

Is there a good time to have sugar?

High-sugar foods can be helpful in some circumstances. When I trained for half-marathons, I'd keep jelly bean packets in my pocket for mid-run fuel. My body could quickly absorb the sugar and use it to keep me running.

If you're an athlete or active person, a handful of candy can give you quick energy if you haven't eaten in a while and it's game time. I'd rather you have some energy than enter a workout on empty.

Again, I reiterate: I do not believe there are "good" and "bad" foods. This includes sugar. But if my goal is to feel and function well, a wide variety of foods is what helps me thrive. This includes some sugar as well as other nutritionally dense foods.

Now if you'll excuse me, I'm going to go have a little chocolate!

Chapter 19

WILL I GAIN WEIGHT IF I EAT SWEET FOODS?

"Will I gain weight if I eat sweet foods?"

No.

Next question.

Wait, you want more than that?

All jokes aside, I understand the question. I even used to think it myself. And there's a good chance you've heard someone enjoy a Crumbl Cookie and proclaim, "now I have to work that off."

Here are two reasons you don't need to "work off" or "earn" sweets or dessert:

1. Sweets math doesn't make you gain weight

First, let's talk about basic math. In 1958, medical researcher Max Wishnofsky, MD, claimed that one pound of adipose (body fat) is equivalent to about 3,500 calories, and a 3,500-calorie deficit is needed to lose one pound of adipose. This has since been debunked, as it oversimplifies our body's dynamic and complex metabolism.[1] But for the sake of putting some numbers together to make a point, let's use that number knowing it's not completely accurate. In this scenario, eating 3,500 calories more than what you need will create one pound of adipose. Desserts vary in caloric content, but let's just say you have a large brownie topped with ice cream that comes in at around 500 calories. You'd have to have seven — *seven!* — of those to gain weight. Those Crumbl cookies are pretty big and average around 800 calories each, but you'd have to have four to gain a pound. I love Crumbl, but not enough to eat four cookies in one sitting!

Personally, I don't feel (or sleep) well if I have dessert every night, so I choose not to. Some families have rituals of dessert every night or once a week. One summer in high school, I remember driving myself and my sister every night to Braum's Ice Cream and Dairy store for a vanilla mix with Oreos. It was a fun ritual that I remember fondly, and I don't remember it impacting my sleep back then. No matter what you decide, when paired with a well-rounded day of quality foods, eating dessert is not going to make you gain weight.

2. "Working off" dessert hurts your relationship with food and exercise

What about the second part of that statement? "I have to work off dessert." A few thoughts on that:

> » *It uses exercise as punishment.* Exercise is something you *get* to do, not something you *have* to do. Don't punish your

body for a decision your brain made. God gave us incredible bodies that move forward, backward, side-to-side, and upside-down. Use that gift to bring joy to your movement, not shame or guilt.

» *It equates to a LOT of exercise.* This varies from person to person, but 500 calories is about the equivalent of walking or running five miles, or about an hour of moderate to intense exercise. All the while, you've got your Inner Mean Girl yelling at you to go longer, faster, harder. This is one of those relationship boundaries it's so important to create within yourself, because the Inner Mean Girl is relentless and will run you until you're hurt.

» *It is a disordered eating thought.* According to the National Eating Disorders Association, disordered eating may include (and is not limited to):

- A rigid food and exercise regime
- Feelings of guilt or shame when unable to maintain that regime
- A preoccupation with food, body, and exercise that has an impact on quality of life
- Compulsive eating
- Compulsive measures to "make up for" food consumed[2]

Disordered eating is the opposite of intuitive eating, which, as dietitian Aaron Flores puts it, allows us to "trust our inner body wisdom and make choices around food that feel good in our body without judgment and without influence from diet culture."[3]

» *It steals the joy of the moment.* What's the purpose of enjoying dessert if we add a serving of shame to it? Decide to have it, savor it, and then put the fork or spoon down when you're satisfied. Save the rest or share with a friend, and tell her I give her permission to enjoy it too.

So all that to say—no, eating dessert *won't* make you gain weight. In fact, I think sitting around the table with people you care about (and who care about you) fits nicely into our CORE Strength. Everything contributes to our health, especially shared memories and experiences while savoring good food with friends and family—so if those shared memories and experiences come with a slice of cake or a scoop of ice cream, I hope you savor it well.

Chapter 20

WHAT'S THE RIGHT WAY TO EAT?

Once upon a time, you were a baby (and I bet you were a pretty cute one!). You pretty much slept, pooped, and ate. You slept when you were tired and pooped when nature called (and I bet if you asked, the people who raised you have some humorous stories of when nature called at the wrong time). When you were hungry, you got fussy or perhaps cried, and when you'd had enough milk, you turned your head away from the bottle or breast.

We were all born with natural eating instincts. Ideally, we keep them. But often, our clear instincts get fuzzy. Well-meaning friends, influencers, diet culture, coaches, health teachers, documentaries, and even parents will teach us not to trust our own bodies and instead set up rigid rules. It's even hard to get online or have a conversation with a group of friends without hearing about the latest or "best" way of eating.

If you've grown up in a health-conscious home, you may want to roll your eyes every time you hear a parent say "you should eat this because it's healthy" (or the opposite, "don't eat that because it's not healthy").

About ten years ago, before I started this journey of ditching diet culture, my own son felt that way. One day, he groaned and said, "Mom, why does everything have to be *healthy* or *unhealthy*? Why can't we just eat the foods we want to eat?" He was right; not everything has to be healthy or unhealthy, because all foods give us energy. But I have to admit, at the time, those words stung. What I had intended as awareness and education turned into a point of tension between us.

Remember, we aren't grading this journey. You're not going to perfectly execute this all the time. I don't either. But here are my five tips on eating to fuel yourself well.

1. Food is a gift, so eat enough

God designed our bodies to need food. We've talked a lot about the different kinds of foods and how they impact how we feel and function. It's up to you to choose which ones work best for you, but the first step is to make sure you're receiving the gift of food.

The nutritionally dense foods in Chapter 12 can help your body thrive. Unfortunately, not everybody has access to these foods. Depending on where you live, your grocery store may primarily stock foods in cans and boxes that can live on the shelf for a while. And sometimes our lifestyles make it hard to have fresh fruits and veggies around. Do what you can with the resources you have.

I'm grateful God gave us the wisdom to package foods in cans and boxes so we can conveniently grab something to give us energy. Today, I got hungry in the middle of writing, but I was on a roll and didn't want to stop for a full lunch break. I grabbed some Cheez-Its and almonds for a quick and easy snack. Later, I'll heat up some leftover chicken fiesta soup to refill my tank for the afternoon.

2. Respond to your body's signals

The same instincts God gave you as a bubbly baby are still with you today—eat when you're hungry and stop when you're satisfied. Save the extras to enjoy later.

Simple to say; harder to do. I get it. I've worked with many teen clients who say, "I don't trust myself to stop." You can and you will; it may just take practice, or maybe even the help of a professional. Don't be afraid to reach out if you need help!

> **Pro Tip:** *It's worth mentioning again that if you need help (re)learning to respond to your signals, check out The Intuitive Eating Workbook for Teens: A Non-Diet, Body-Positive Approach to Building a Healthy Relationship with Food by Elyse Resch.*

3. Fill your plate with a variety of foods

Let's be honest; none of us are going to do this every single time we eat. I certainly don't. Just try to balance out your day and think of it from a zoomed-out lens rather than worrying about every. Single. Thing. Did you have a cheeseburger and fries for lunch? How about giving your body some different nutrients in your next meal by including some fruit and a veggie you enjoy?

Eat when you're hungry and stop when you're satisfied.

Imagine your plate divided into quarters. Try to fill each quarter with a protein, a fruit, a veggie, and a grain. Add a side of dairy to get calcium (and some extra protein, if it's cow's milk).

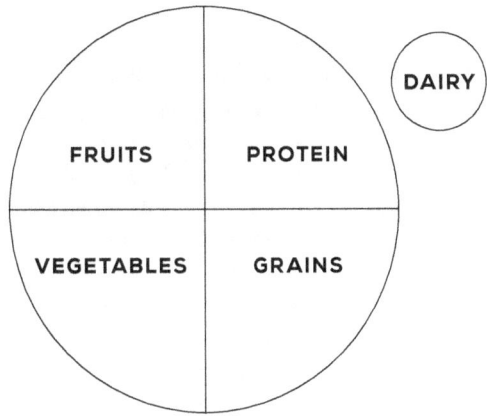

Pro Tip: *You can snack on items you may be missing out on in your main meals.*

4. Don't skip meals

When I travel to visit family members who live seven hours away, I always head out with a full tank of gas. I want to make sure I have plenty of fuel to get to where I'm going. If I run out of gas, my car won't go.

Your body, and especially your brain, need to be fueled up before school. Like I said in Chapter 17, your brain gets its energy from carbs. When you don't eat anything at all, your brain is trying to learn on empty. And just like I stop for gas halfway between my home in Houston and my parents' house in Oklahoma, you need to refuel during lunch. Don't skip lunch, even if those around you do. Show them what it's like to honor your body and respond to its request for more fuel.

Even if you've had a large meal the night before, please still eat a little something in the morning. It doesn't have to be huge, but get a little carb, protein, and fat in your system. Breakfast cookies and breakfast cookie bowls are staples in our mornings. Both recipes are in the Resource Guide.

5. Stay hydrated

Putting fluids in your body helps it feel and function well. And as we will discuss in Chapter 29, it's important for your bowel movements. Refer back to Chapter 14 for hacks for those who don't like the taste of water.

As I learned to let my boys choose their own foods while still helping them identify how those foods made them feel, I didn't hear the groans as much. Both of my boys now have a solid understanding of what makes their bodies feel and function well. Does that mean they always abide by that? No. Again, I don't either. But knowing is truly half the battle, and now our whole family is empowered to make decisions for ourselves.

Chapter 21

HOW SHOULD I WARM UP?

We're entering the part of this book that talks more about movement. What better way to do that than with a chapter on warming up?

I'm the kind of person who needs to wake up slowly before I get going with my day. I'm not ready to talk to anyone, and I'm *certainly* not ready to think hard about anything. I need to spend time with God and His Word in quiet solitude. Sadly, I get a bit cranky when this is interrupted, which I guess means I just need more Jesus!

I need to warm up in the mornings, and I need to warm up before a workout. If I don't, my body gets cranky — or worse, injured.

When exercising, the purpose of the warm-up is to prepare your body for physical activity. There are three main points of interest in a warm-up:

1. **Prepare your heart and lungs** for your workout and get them working faster to accommodate your moving body. It can take a few minutes to do this, which is why that first

part can feel so hard. When I taught indoor cycling classes, I always felt a little sheepish being out of breath so early on. Thirty minutes into the workout, however, I could verbalize the cues without feeling so winded.

2. **Stretch your muscles** so they will move the way you want them to without getting injured. There are a few ways to do this in the warm-up:

    - *Self-myofascial release (SMR).* SMR, otherwise known as foam rolling, involves moving your muscles along a roller to release dense muscle fibers, or knots. SMR can also help your connective tissue. It is particularly helpful for those really tight areas.

    - *Dynamic stretching.* This type of stretch uses continual movement and momentum to move a joint through its full range of motion. Dynamic stretching is what we do when we squat, lunge, reach, and push our way through the beginning of a workout.

3. **Activate the muscles** you're going to use. This basically turns them on and says "get ready to move" so they work best.

    Have you ever had someone bump into you when you weren't expecting it? You were probably taken off guard and may have stumbled or fallen. But if you know someone is coming, you can brace yourself and your muscles can be ready for the impact.

    Turning on your muscles prepares them for moving and

keeps them from getting injured. In almost every scenario, you can't go wrong with glute bridges and some bear crawls.

> **Pro Tip:** *If your workout involves leaving the ground, especially if you're an athlete who runs and/or jumps (soccer, volleyball, basketball, softball… pretty much any sport), I beg you to spend some time warming up your smaller glute muscles, or what I call "mini muscles." This includes loop walks, glute bridges (I'm a huge fan of them, even though they feel super awkward), clamshells, and glute pumps. Strengthening these muscles will support your knees and help prevent you from sustaining ACL, MCL, or meniscus injuries that can sideline you for weeks.*

Because it's easier to watch and learn rather than read and learn, check out the Resource Guide, where I've provided links to several YouTube videos I've made on warming up. I have videos showing SMR, dynamic stretching, and warming up your mini muscles in the Pro Tip above.

You may notice I did not include static stretching in the warm-up. Static stretching is when we take a stretch and hold it for twenty to thirty seconds. This releases what's called the Golgi tendon organ and relaxes the muscle, which is not what we want before we exercise, as this can cause injury and decreased performance. Save your static stretching for the cool-down or for an active recovery day (both discussed in future chapters).

Consider the warm-up as an investment in your activity. If you take the time to prepare your heart, lungs, and muscles, they'll work better for you in your workout and in the future.

Chapter 22

HOW DO I CREATE A WORKOUT THAT'S BEST FOR ME?

was recently chatting with one of my son's friends, and she mentioned that she was heading to the gym later that day. Always curious (and only sometimes nosy!), I asked what kind of workout she planned to do.

"Honestly, I typically just do whatever I find on TikTok," she said.

Fair enough. I know of highly respected educators on social media who help us move well. We can find workouts, recipes, and cooking tips with a few swipes, all lasting sixty seconds or less.

While these clips are helpful, I'd like you to understand the foundation of working out. And I want you to be able to design your own workout because you know it's best for *you*, not because the latest influencer recommended it.

You can find a million different ways to move your body. Some require more flexibility than others; some require more strength. Some are creative; others are simple. Some are just flat-out crazy impressive. One of these days, I'm hoping to be able to properly replicate some of the impressive shots from the Athleta fitness clothing magazines. It's unlikely, though.

We all have different ways we like to move our body. You may not be interested in strength training right now. If so, skip past that section. I want you to exercise because you enjoy it, not because you feel like you have to.

If you're ready to play around with strength training and you're at home, first find some space. At a minimum, you'll need enough room to fit a yoga mat, but ideally, you'll have a bit more.

Now, let's discuss putting together a workout—no TikTok needed.

Basic movements you need to know

Functional movements, in which we mimic actual movements, utilize several muscles at once (they're great for calorie-burning as well, if that's a goal of yours). They also reduce the tendency to overdevelop muscles, which can cause imbalance or injury (which *should* be a goal of yours). Functional movements fall into one of six categories:

1. **Push:** Pushing involves moving your hands away from you to the front or overhead. *(Push-up)*

2. **Pull:** Pulling involves moving your hands or legs toward your body from the front or from an overhead position. *(Pulling weight back like a row)*

3. **Squat:** Your feet are in contact with the ground and your hips flex while they draw down closer to your feet. (*Basic squat*)

4. **Hinge:** Hinging occurs mostly in your hips. Just like a door hinge has a moving part (the door) and a stabilizing unit (the frame), your upper body can hinge downward (the door) while your legs stay straight (the frame). (*Bending over at your hips like a Romanian deadlift*)

5. **Lunge/single leg:** One foot leaves the ground while the other leg does the work. (*Stepping up on a box*)

6. **Rotational movements:** These involve rotating either your thoracic spine (which is your middle back) or your pelvis. (*Spinal twist*)

What do I do with these basic movements?

Find a few movements you like in each category and rotate through them. Ideally, follow a pattern that uses opposing movements. Push, then pull. Or squat, then rotate. Not only does this create balance in your body but it also prevents overtraining particular muscles.

If you're not sure which category each exercise falls under, or even what to do, I've provided plenty of answers in the Resource Guide.

How many reps should I do?

I recommend starting with eight to ten repetitions of any movement. If you fly through them and finish the tenth rep without any difficulty, it's time to add more reps or increase your weight by ten percent.

What about my biceps?

Crowd favorites like biceps curls, crunches, and triceps extensions get a lot of playing time on social media. Those focus on what I call "beach muscles." I'm not going to name any names, but check out a beach pic of a group of guys. Chances are they're all crossing their arms and puffing up their biceps with their hands while simultaneously contracting their abdomens. They're probably flexing their pectorals (chest muscles) as well. These are beach muscles. I get why they're doing it, but it doesn't mean you aren't strong if you don't have those particular muscles. Additionally, when you perform functional movements, you'll often strengthen these beach muscles as well as less obvious muscles.

Should I take a rest day?

While strength training is helpful, it is possible to have too much of a good thing. Allow your muscles forty-eight hours in between strength sessions to allow for repair and recovery. Factor in rest days. And make sure you sleep enough to allow your body to grow those muscles back.

Do I need a rest day if I'm not strength training?

That depends on what you do. If you have a hard sprint workout, definitely take it down a notch the next day. But if your joy comes from running at a moderate pace every day, you can go two to three days without a rest day. Listen and respond to what your body needs.

What else can I do besides strength training?

I know I've focused a lot on strength training here. This seems to be the most confusing aspect of exercising to women of all ages. We'll cover a few reasons why it's a great way to work out in the next chapter.

But if you want to do something other than strength training, then do it! There are other ways of working out, so let's briefly cover them here:

» **Cardio**: Cardiovascular training, otherwise known as "cardio," encompasses any activity that raises your heart rate for an extended period of time. Walking, running, swimming, and biking are all great examples of cardio. This absolutely has a place in a well-rounded workout routine, and if you have a choice between doing cardio and doing nothing, definitely do cardio. Just be aware that while cardio is great for strengthening your heart, you're somewhat limited on how much muscle you can build with these workouts.

» **Mind/Body**: Yoga, Pilates, Tai Chi, and even my signature class, B.COMPLETE, all reside under the mind/body category. These are all wonderful ways to move your body, strengthen your core, and improve your flexibility and range of motion. Because they only use your body weight and not external "toys" like weights or resistance, I'm giving you the green light to follow along on TikTok, YouTube, Instagram, or another platform. Just make sure they are the appropriate level for you and your body. (Interested in B.COMPLETE? Find more info in the Resource Guide.)

» **Dance/Fitness Fusion:** Group fitness classes that use dance moves as the foundation of a workout are a fun way to joyfully move. Check out classes like Zumba, UJam, Pound Fitness, and Jazzercise, all of which combine choreography and upbeat music to dance your way through the class.

Play around with the different types of workouts and put together your own. Then, when you follow along with your favorite TikTok fitness guru, you'll know if what they are guiding you to do is beneficial or if they are just focused on beach muscles but not much more (or promoting their own agenda that may not be best for you!).

Finally, remember our CORE Strength: *We take care of our original bodies in a variety of ways so we can do what we are called to do.* We just need to feel and function well enough to be physically able to live out the days, weeks, months, and years God has in store for us.

Chapter 23

WHY SHOULD I STRENGTH TRAIN?

I know I've picked on TikTok and Instagram a lot in this book. I'm not even sure if I should apologize for that. But I will say one positive thing about social media: it shows the benefits of all kinds of exercise, including strength training.

If you want to try strength training, hooray! Please do. But have you thought about *why* you should want to strength train beyond getting stronger? Here are a few lesser-known reasons to lift heavy things:

Fix or prevent "tech neck"

Have you ever found yourself reaching back to massage your tender neck or upper shoulders? There's a good possibility you can thank your phone for that if you're hunched over looking at it all day. Maybe you get headaches or even muscle pain, numbness, or tingling in your neck, back, or shoulder.

As the meme says, we are all turning into question marks. Standing with poor posture or sitting at a computer with your head thrust forward causes increased strain on your neck and back. The more you tilt your head down, the greater the strain on your neck and upper spine, as well as the muscles and ligaments that support them.

Resistance training—specifically pulling exercises—can help strengthen your neck and back muscles. Since I haven't taken the time and energy to master more than one and a half pull-ups (they are SO HARD!), I've found resistance bands and loops to be incredibly beneficial for this. You'll find a video with pulling exercises in the Resource Guide.

Improve your athletic performance

If you're an athlete, strong muscles will improve your performance. I hope your coaches include some sort of strength training in your programming. We covered some of the basics of strength training in Chapter 22, so if you're ready to take your athletics to the next level and are not currently strength training, utilize the resources at the end of that chapter.

As I mentioned in a previous Pro Tip, if your sport of choice involves leaving the ground, like track, cross country, volleyball, basketball, or softball, I highly recommend that you spend some time strengthening what I call the "mini muscles." These are the smaller muscles around your hips that support your movement. Specifically, they support the movement of your femur, or thigh bone, and keep it in proper alignment with your knee.

When we have weak mini muscles, the femur can shift out of place when you land, resulting in the dreaded ACL, MCL, or meniscus tear. You can have strong and powerful quads, calves, hamstrings, and gluteus maximus (the big muscles in your butt), but if those mini muscles are weak, you're still at risk for injury. Look for a quick mini muscle workout in the Resource Guide.

Prevent your spine from curving and your hips from breaking later in life

Did you know that peak bone mass for women is around age twenty-six? After that, it's difficult to strengthen your bones. Osteoporosis, or the breakdown of bone, is probably not on your radar right now, but if you'll indulge me for this one section, I'd like you to think about your future self's bones.

Your bone health is dependent on many factors, including what you eat, how much calcium and vitamin D you get, and how active you are. We've covered some of the nutritional aspects already, so let's zero in on activity.

Basically, any time you generate pressure on your bones and joints, this kind of training helps strengthen them. Higher-impact activities like walking, running, and jumping are great for the lower part of your body, but we can't forget about the upper body. Pulling exercises like dumbbell rows, band pull-downs, and bent-over rows with any kind of weight can help promote bone growth in your spine.

Chances are you already have a full set of permanent teeth. You know these are the same teeth that will be with you for the rest of your life. The same is true of your bones. The development they undergo until your mid-twenties is basically what is going to support you for your time on earth. If we continually skip brushing our teeth (gross, please don't do this), we get cavities. And if we don't strengthen our bones, they won't be able to withstand the inevitable weakening that happens after menopause.

Resistance training for your bone health now is like brushing and flossing every day for your dental health. You may not see the immediate benefits, but it will pay off in the long run.

Manage diabetes

A friend of mine has Type 1 diabetes and has worked out with me in the past. She patiently answers my questions about her insulin pump, glucose levels, and more. Because she tracks her blood sugar and knows I'm curious, she told me that her blood sugar levels are much better when she strength trains. Her report was anecdotal, but the research supports this for both Type 1 and Type 2 diabetes.[1]

If you or a loved one have Type 2 diabetes and have been told to control your blood sugar, strength training can help with this.

Increase your metabolism

I hope by now we've established that I come from a weight-neutral perspective, and I hope you're joining me in that perspective. But I also know that there are times when taking care of ourselves will result in body composition changes. Strength training can help your resting metabolic rate (RMR), otherwise known as your metabolism. Your RMR churns along whether you are sitting in class, sleeping, or scrolling. RMR is the amount of energy your body needs to sustain life. The more muscle you have, the higher your metabolism, which can help your body composition.

Increase your confidence

I think this can apply to any type of movement, but there's something extra special that comes along with strength training: confidence. The confidence we earn in the gym ripples out to other areas of our lives.

Knowing we can lift and move heavy things helps us stand a little taller (literally and figuratively). Personally, I like being able to decline offers to help me move large objects because I know I can do it without assistance.

> Grocery bagger: "Would you like help taking these bags of ice to the car?"
>
> Me, grabbing four 8-pound bags: "Nope! This is why I work out!"

Even if you don't have any resistance equipment, you have your amazing body. I've included a video of simple bodyweight movements in the Resource Guide.

After you've been strength training a while, try increasing your resistance. Grab a tougher band. Go up ten percent in dumbbells. Get the heavier kettlebell. And if you've never done strength training, now is the time to try it. See what happens. You may find yourself pleasantly surprised at what you can handle.

Chapter 24

HOW DO I STRENGTHEN MY CORE?

(Admit it... you're thinking, Finally!
We are talking about strengthening my core!)

Every summer for five years, I ran teen fitness classes outside at my local multipurpose fields. I'd have each participant fill out an intake form so I could understand their goals, their fitness level coming into classes, and what was important to them.

Without fail, they all wanted to strengthen their cores.

This is also the goal of clients who are my age. And young men. And older men. And older women. Everyone, it seems, wants to strengthen their cores.

To this, I say, YES! (Also: YES to our CORE Strength, as discussed in Part One.) But what does that really mean?

Why do I want a strong core?

Think of your body as a tree. The branches are like your arms, legs, and head, while the trunk and roots represent your core (which, coincidentally, is also called a "trunk"). If a tree's trunk and roots are strong and stable, it can withstand pressure like wind and storms. Without a strong trunk and roots, the tree can topple over in a strong storm or hurricane (trust me on this; we lost several trees in Hurricane Harvey).

Your core acts as the foundation of everything you do. It stabilizes you, protects your organs, and acts as your center of gravity. A strong core will also help you:

- » Sit up straighter
- » Stay balanced
- » Perform better athletically
- » Reduce your chance of injury

Core ≠ Six-Pack Abs

Having a strong core does not mean automatically developing six-pack abs. Your core is a combination of over twenty muscle groups that work together. It's basically all the muscles that run from just below your bra line to below your rear. Your core is not one muscle but rather a region of your body that controls the motion of your pelvis, femurs, rib cage, and spine.

Which exercises will strengthen my core?

Oh friend, my mind is swimming with all the possibilities of what to write here. But to start, here are five exercises that are sure to strengthen your core when done correctly:

- » Glute bridges
- » Elbow planks
- » Dead bugs
- » Floor prone cobras
- » Bird dogs

Believe it or not, many of the functional movements we discussed in Chapter 22 also strengthen your core. Examples of these functional movements that have dual purpose include:

- » Squats
- » Deadlifts
- » Turkish get-ups
- » Renegade rows
- » Medicine ball slams

Pro Tip: *If you're going to slam a medicine ball, make sure it's the kind that will stay grounded and not bounce back up and slam you in the face. Ouch.*

I've included two videos about this in the Resource Guide. One goes through my five recommended core exercises and shows proper form. Even if you think you have proper form, it's worth watching just to make sure. The second video is a ten-minute core workout. Do this workout on its own or as part of a longer workout.

Your core acts as the foundation of everything you do.

What about crunches or sit-ups?

Meh. These aren't bad, per se, but they only work your rectus abdominus (that six-pack). It's more worthwhile to do them as long as you do other exercises to holistically strengthen your core, like the five listed above.

Strengthening your core is definitely worth your workout time. Just make sure you also spend time on your CORE Strength and remember why: *We take care of our original bodies in a variety of ways so we can do what we are called to do.* Strengthen your CORE and your core to stay strong and stand tall in all of life's storms.

Chapter 25

HOW LONG SHOULD I WORK OUT?

One of my son's friends has a sister who trains as a gymnast. After a full day of school, she heads to the gymnasium, where she trains for three to four hours. She heads home for homework and sleep, then rinses and repeats every weekday.

Competitive gymnasts are known for their intense training regimens, and I admire the work and dedication they put in. Athletes in all sports know that hard work pays off, and many will invest extra time doing the hard work. But if I'm honest, I'm not interested in putting in that kind of time in my own life and workouts. Long workouts are not necessary to live a healthy, holistic lifestyle.

Let's assume you're like me and just want to take care of yourself and then go about your day. Then what?

How long should my workouts be?

The lower the intensity of the workout, the longer you can exercise. (Notice I said *can*. That doesn't mean you have to.) The higher the intensity, the shorter the workout should be. Why? Because your body uses different energy sources, and you'll quickly run out of the one that fuels high intensity, which is called ATP, short for adenosine triphosphate (you can see why we use the shortened version!).

Here's a quick-reference general guide for workout lengths depending on intensity:

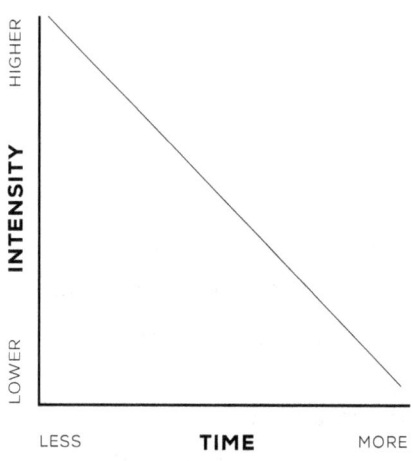

INTENSITY	EXAMPLES	RECOMMENDED MAX TIME
Low	slow walking, parade-pace bicycling, gentle yoga, stretching	As long as you are enjoying it
Moderate	faster walking, jogging, swimming, yoga, hiking, elliptical/stair machine, strength training	Up to sixty minutes
High	anything that makes you breathless, like sprints, jump squats, or box jumps	Twenty to thirty minutes (taking breaks in between sets)

This is rough guidance and will change based on your goals and fitness level, but it's a good rule of thumb to follow.

Can I work out twice in one day?

If we were sitting across from each other having coffee, I'd want to ask more questions before giving you an answer.

» Why do you want to work out more than once per day?

» What kinds of workouts are you doing?

» Are you fueling well in between?

» Are you getting plenty of sleep?

If you want to work out twice per day because you're trying to lose weight and you're also restricting your nutrition, I'd discourage you. In fact, I'd *beg* you not to do this. Doing intense two-a-days and not eating as much is a recipe for burnout and possible injury, and it can lead to an eating disorder.

When I was running more and participating in half marathons, there were always T-shirts at the merch tent that said "eat sleep run repeat." If you're going to *run* and then *repeat*, you must *eat* and *sleep* enough to support that.

I'd rather see you consistently do one workout a few times a week than do two-a-days for a week and then burn out and stop altogether. And I highly discourage two-a-days if you're just starting out. Just like I had to work up to running a 13.1-mile half marathon, your body needs to work up to exercising twice in one day.

Honestly, I just don't think it's worth the time or energy to do two-a-days, but you know your body best.

What if I only have a few minutes to squeeze in a workout?

My high school chemistry teacher was engaging and quite eccentric. My now-husband and I happened to be in the same chemistry class and had this teacher together (though we were just friends at the time). To this day, we still recall her antics through tear-filled laughter.

I don't remember much about what I learned (chemistry was *so hard* for me!), but I do remember when that teacher encouraged us to take short pockets of time to study. "Just five minutes will make a difference in what you can learn," she told us.

She was right, and I'll say the same to you. Just five, ten, or twenty minutes makes a difference. You can absolutely get a good workout in twenty minutes. I know; I do it all the time. In my house, we say it this way: *Something is better than nothing.*

By the way, if you're a competitive athlete, this chapter may not be for you, but sock it away for future reference anyway, because for most people (except basketball GOAT LeBron James, who might still be dunking when he's eighty), there will be a day when you transition from competitive to recreational sports, and you may want to reference this.

So how long should you exercise? The answer is a bit fuzzy, but one thing is clear: listen to your body and give yourself the fuel and sleep you need in addition to exercise.

Chapter 26

WHY DO I THROW UP DURING OR AFTER MY WORKOUT?

High school cross country meets are not for the faint of heart, and I'm not even talking about the athletes. Obviously the athletes work hard. In fact, those who compete by running cross country like to boast that their sport of running is punishment for other sports.

But come to a cross country meet early in the season, especially in my hot and humid area, and you'll see what I mean. Just past the finish line are young men and women who have finished their race, hunched over with their hands on their knees. Normal, right? Yes. But they're also vomiting. Everywhere. Common, but not normal. I've even seen athletes toss their chins over their shoulders while sprinting to the finish line and eject the contents of their stomach as they run. Ick.

Every four years, I gleefully anticipate the Summer Olympics. I especially appreciate watching events in which I've participated as a recreational athlete. My personal times compared to the times of these best-of-the-best women help me understand just how impressive they are.

But look closely and think about it: have you ever seen Allyson Felix complete her 400-meter run and then vomit? What about Katie Ledecky after her 400-meter swim? These inspirational women have each earned seven Olympic gold medals. Zero times have they finished and immediately thrown up on international television.

If it's not normal for the highest-caliber athletes to vomit after their workouts, why do we think this is okay for us?

It's not. Throwing up during or after a workout may be common, but it's not normal. In fact, it's often a sign that something is off. Assuming you have no medical issues, consider one of these four reasons that you may vomit during or after a workout:

1. You aren't hydrated

Sure, your school may allow you to bring water bottles, but do you drink from it enough throughout the day? Aim for at least sixty-four ounces per day, but if you are outside or sweating a lot, you may need more.

As I mentioned in Chapter 14, you can get a good idea of your hydration level by the color of your urine. Darker = dehydrated, lighter = hydrated.

But don't drink an entire day's worth of water at one time! Have you ever tried to water a plant with extremely dry soil? The water runs straight through, and the plant doesn't absorb anything. That's pretty much what happens with your body. Your organs, connective tissue, and blood need a light, steady stream of water to best absorb your fluids, not a last-minute chug before practice or at the end of the day.

2. Your electrolyte levels are off

Electrolytes balance the fluid levels in our cells and throughout our bodies so they can run optimally. Electrolytes come from food and fluids, and the main ones include sodium, potassium, magnesium, and calcium. Unfortunately, many Americans under-consume electrolyte-rich foods and may not get enough, with the exception of sodium. Sodium is a common ingredient added to many foods, so we typically consume more than enough of it.

When we sweat a lot, we lose a lot of electrolytes. If you've ever discovered a white line on your black sports bra or hat after a hard workout, it means you've lost a lot of electrolytes through your sweat and you need to focus on replenishing them with specific foods. Here are some foods to help ensure you're getting enough potassium, magnesium, and calcium (since we generally get enough sodium, I won't include that):

- » Potassium: bananas; dried apricots; spinach; sweet potatoes; avocados
- » Magnesium: wheat bran; spinach; Brazil nuts; cashews; quinoa; flax seeds; pumpkin seeds; sunflower seeds; dark chocolate; avocadoes; wheat bread
- » Calcium: dairy products like yogurt, milk and cheese; leafy greens; tofu; fortified plant-based milk (you may find milk is better consumed after a workout rather than right before)

If you're exercising hard or in intense heat, you may need to supplement with some electrolyte drinks. Here are a few guidelines if you do:

» Look at the label. Specifically look for potassium and magnesium. Since sodium is an electrolyte, some sports drinks throw a bunch of sodium into a bottle and call it an electrolyte. The added sodium is not bad, but you may need more than just salt.

» Experiment with when you drink it. I find having it as a replenishment after my workout feels best, but you may want to have it before or even during.

3. You've eaten too much too close to when you exercise

What you eat and when you eat it can impact how your stomach feels during exercise. You may have to do a personal science experiment on this, as everyone tolerates food and exercise differently.

In general, the closer you are to your workout time, the more carbs you want to consume because they are easier to digest. Consume higher-fat foods a few hours prior to exercise or after, but not right before.

For example, it's 3 p.m. and you have a 4 p.m. soccer game. It's been several hours since lunch, and dinner won't be until after the game. Here are some ideas for how to fuel up without weighing your belly down:

» Banana and peanut butter
» Turkey sandwich
» String cheese and grapes

- » Toasted English muffin with almond butter and sliced pears, peaches, or apples
- » Dried apricots and almonds

4. Your Inner Mean Girl is pushing you too much

One of my former teen clients came to me to meet a running goal as part of her athletics program. Her middle school coach told them, "you're going to run until you throw up." This client loathed running, and this coach's messaging certainly didn't help.

When I heard this story, I cringed. I wish some coaches could see the impacts of their words. This kind of language fails to respect your body and how you feel.

What about the Inner Mean Girl Coach in your head who yells, "harder, faster, more, more, more!" What does she want for you? Is she punishing you for eating dessert... not exercising enough... your tight-fitting pants?

You may not be able to fire your athletic coach, but you can certainly fire the mean one in your head. Look for a new coach who allows mistakes in food timing, but learns from those mistakes... who gently reminds you to drink your water throughout the day... who always treats you with grace.

《 》

Yes, getting sick during or after a workout happens from time to time. There's no shame in this, and the reason can be as simple as drinking more water earlier in the day or eating something lighter right before a workout. God gave you an amazing body and a bright brain; use these and the tools in this chapter to experiment with what works best for you.

Chapter 27

HOW SHOULD I COOL DOWN?

What would you say if I told you that your next workout begins at the end of your current one? Believe it or not, one of the best times to improve your performance is during the recovery time between sweat sessions.

This includes the time you invest (and it truly is an investment) in cooling down as well as in your nutrition and sleep. I confess: I haven't always been great at cooling down, but I make myself do it now because my body feels so much better when I do.

Just like a warm-up, a cool-down (or warm-down, as some coaches call it) has two components: bringing your heart rate down and elongating the muscles you just worked.

I often refer to the cool-down period as putting your body back together. After the adjustments it makes to get the workout done, it needs to get back to its normal physiological state. We also need to prepare for whatever is next on our to-do list.

So, specifically, how should I cool down?

Depending on your goals and how you're feeling, you can try some different approaches:

» **Slow down.** If you've been on a fast walk or run, take the last few minutes to decrease your pace. Then, ideally, add in at least one of the next three suggestions.

» **Focus on mobility.** Mobility offers you the benefits of joint stability, increased range of motion, and moving your body differently than the way you just moved it during the workout. It's typically lower intensity, so it's a great two-for-one in a cooldown.

» **Stretch.** Now is also the time to utilize static stretching, or stretches you hold for thirty seconds or more. Dynamic stretching (as discussed in Chapter 21) is also appropriate. Focus on the muscles you used the most that day or those that need some extra attention. (And if you need to hold a stretch longer than a coach or fitness instructor is calling for, by all means, do it.)

» **Try self-myofascial release.** Also known as foam rolling, this is appropriate as a cool-down as well as a warm-up.

How long should I cool down?

Plan on at least five minutes.

Cooling down is also a great way of saying "thank you" to your body for moving the way you asked it to. Check in with how everything feels. Respond to that.

The most effective workouts include time for your body to ramp up and also put itself back together. When you take this time, you'll decrease your chance of injury and set yourself up for another strong workout.

Chapter 28

WHY DO I NEED A REST DAY? WHAT SHOULD I DO?

A couple years ago, my son came downstairs ready to head to the gym sporting a new tank top that said "No Days Off." I try hard not to make unwanted comments about their food and exercise (and fail often), so on this occasion, I didn't say anything, but my eyes betrayed me. He watched my gaze drift from his face down to his tank. He knew me well enough to know I was cringing on the inside.

"I know you hate this shirt, Mom," he said, "but it was on sale, and I like to wear tanks to the gym."

That, my friend, is what I call a mom win. He knew where I stood and addressed it. As a bonus, he had used his money wisely and purchased it on sale!

The slogan "No Days Off," though, is *not* a win.

Why does my body need a rest day?

When you exercise, your muscles develop microtears. In order for your muscles to rebuild, they need to have some down time. During this time, your blood replenishes and repairs the microtears by delivering oxygen and nutrients to your muscles.

If you constantly place your muscles and systems under exercise stress, they can't receive the elements needed for their growth and repair. Skipping recovery days skips the growth. This is why it's important to schedule at least one rest day (also called recovery day).

How long should I rest my muscles?

The general consensus among fitness professionals is to allow forty-eight hours in between working the same muscle groups. For example, if you do pushing and pulling exercises for your upper body on Monday, avoid taxing those same muscles until Wednesday. On Tuesday, you can focus on your lower body.

As a rule of thumb, if certain muscles are still sore from your previous workout but it's been forty-eight hours, you can still exercise them. Just ensure that it has, indeed, been a full two days.

What should I do on a recovery day?

Honestly, this is going to be different for everyone. The key is to move gently if you choose to move. Gentle movement, rather than a couch-based Netflix binge, is helpful for getting the nutrients to your muscles.

Here are some ideas:

- » Prayer walk (Casually walk down your street or neighborhood specifically praying for each family)
- » Yoga
- » Mobility
- » Self-Myofascial Release/foam rolling
- » Bike ride (think parade pace, not race pace)
- » Nap
- » B.COMPLETE, my signature program
- » Stretch

Are there other benefits to a rest day?

I especially love rest days because they encourage me to take it easy. I get a little extra time in my morning, and quite honestly, I like the mental break. Let's be honest: Figuring out how and when to move, what to eat, and how to successfully execute all of this amid an already full day is exhausting. Physically, yes, but mentally as well. Even as a lifelong fitness enthusiast, I feel a little mentally lighter on the days I previously scheduled rest. And the best part? It's doing exactly what God modeled after creating light, water, sky, land, planets, stars, creatures, and man (see Genesis 2:2–3). If God took a rest day, I should too!

But I really don't think I need one!

I'm going to push back on this. When your muscles are taxed beyond their ability to recover, they act out in the form of overtraining syndrome. In other words, you get hurt. This shows up as muscle strains, stress fractures, joint pain, and more.

Need more encouragement? Pull up your Bible app and search for the word "rest." You'll see all the places God demonstrates, offers, and even commands rest. My favorite is in Mark 6:31, when Jesus said to His disciples, "Come with me by yourselves to a quiet place and get some rest." If Jesus modeled rest, then I believe He wanted us to do it as well.

Give your body the rest it needs to grow physically and spiritually. And for goodness' sake, take a day off, even if a tank top tells you not to!

If Jesus modeled rest then I believe He wanted us to do it as well.

Chapter 29

WHY CAN'T I POOP?

Once I had a mom reach out to me in confidence about her daughter, who was a client of mine. "She would die of embarrassment if she knew I told you this, but she's been having a lot of pooping issues and constipation lately."

Little did that mom know that she was not the first — or the last — person to share this with me.

How can I poop better?

If you're dealing with similar pooping issues, you're not alone. Often this is remedied by doing three things:

1. Drink more water (like we've said, aim for sixty-four ounces or more per day)
2. Choose foods high in fiber
3. Eat enough food to provide energy for all you do

Simple enough, but sometimes it's harder to actually implement. Let's back up a bit and talk about why we need fiber, what foods have it, and how to deal with constipation.

What does fiber have to do with pooping?

Focusing on fiber isn't just for old people! I mean, this isn't exactly the most exciting topic, and I certainly don't expect it to be in your Snapchat stories, but regardless of how old you are, fiber can make a huge difference in how your body feels, functions, and, yes, poops.

How much do you need? Females need about twenty-five grams of fiber per day. Most Americans only get fifteen grams per day, meaning we are missing out on the secret superpower of fiber.[1]

Fiber is the unsung hero of our digestive system. Fiber can:

» Help you feel fuller for longer

» Help control blood sugar and reduce potential blood sugar spikes (super helpful for not falling asleep in class!)

» Promote bowel health (my client's mom confirmed that she wasn't getting enough fiber)[2]

» Promote a strong gut microbiome, which helps regulate things like your immune system and mental health[3]

How do I get fiber (especially if I don't like vegetables)?

Foods like leafy green vegetables, broccoli, and Brussels sprouts all are high in fiber. I had to grow into liking these foods, so if those make your face scrunch up, I get it. It takes time. Just keep trying, and try new ways of preparing these foods.

A good rule of thumb is that if something is a plant, it likely has fiber. I'm probably going to sound a bit redundant here, but eating plants in their natural state (and the way God gave them to us) is a wonderful way to get fiber.

The good news is that plenty of other plants (not just vegetables!) are high in fiber. Here are a few high-fiber plants that aren't vegetables:

- Chickpeas (½ cup = 5 grams)
- Chia seeds (1 tablespoon = 4 grams)
- Avocados (½ medium avocado = 5 grams)
- Oats (¾ cup = 6 grams)
- Black beans (½ cup = 6 grams)
- Flaxseed (1 tablespoon = 3 grams)
- Popcorn (3 cups = 4 grams)
- Blueberries (1 cup = 4 grams)
- Raspberries (1 cup = 8 grams)
- Blackberries (1 cup = 8 grams)

Pro Tip: *Drink plenty of water with your fiber-rich foods. Fiber needs water to activate its superpowers. If your system doesn't have enough water to absorb, then you won't get fiber's benefits.*

Pro Tip: *Increase your fiber intake slowly to allow your body to get used to it.*

What about fiber supplements?

Before you go this route, I encourage you to try the three suggestions above: drink more water, choose high fiber foods, and eat enough. This will often remedy your problem. Ask yourself the easiest and most realistic way to get more fiber. Perhaps it's eating more fruit, snacking on chickpeas, or having a high-fiber breakfast like overnight oats with chia seeds.

In some cases determined by you and your doctor, over-the-counter fiber supplements may be beneficial. Do this under a physician or dietitian's guidance.

How can I avoid becoming constipated?

When you regularly consume plenty of fiber, water, and food in general, your bowel movements will become more regular. A bonus to this is that your body will learn the optimal times to poop. Let's be honest—no one wants to poop during a passing period at school in a potentially icky school bathroom. Likewise, an early morning sporting event may be lined with port-o-potties (it can be a toss-up which is worse: school bathrooms or portable toilets). Giving your body what it needs most days will often lead to your body feeling safe enough to "go" at times that work for you, like before or after school.

For what it's worth, I've peed and pooped in more public restrooms and port-o-potties than I can count. It's awkward and uncomfortable, but it's more uncomfortable when I don't listen and respond to my body. Besides, we are all human. It's like the book that was likely read to us when we were three: *Everybody Poops*. Even Jesus was fully human, so you know what that means. (If I could insert an emoji here, it would be the poop one. Obviously.)

What if I have the opposite problem and have diarrhea often?

Diarrhea's cause is not the opposite of constipation. Getting too much fiber will not bring about diarrhea unless you've completely overloaded your system. Instead, it may point to other reasons:

- » A food intolerance or allergy
- » Consumption of too much fatty food
- » Overeating, causing your digestive system to be overwhelmed
- » Overconsumption of alcohol or caffeine
- » Medications like antibiotics, which are helpful in killing bacteria but unfortunately also rid your digestive system of good bacteria

> **Pro Tip:** *If you're on antibiotics, consume fermented foods like yogurt, kefir, kombucha kimchi, miso, and sourdough bread to help restore your gut microbiome.*

There are other medical reasons for consistent diarrhea. Please contact a physician if you can't manage diarrhea.

Fiber probably isn't something you sit around the lunch table discussing, but if you can add one high-fiber serving a day, you'll be on your way to feeling great all the way through (another bad pun… permission to roll your eyes at that one!).

> **Pro Tip:** *Most of the recipes in the back of the book are also high in fiber, so if you're looking for something new with plenty of fiber, give them a try.*

Chapter 30

HOW CAN I LOSE WEIGHT? SHOULD I? DO I NEED TO?

I showed up for my annual doctor check-up and stepped on the scale. I looked to the side as the number displayed because I wasn't in the mood to play head games with an arbitrary number. The medical assistant wrote it down and led me into the exam room to wait for my doctor. Unfortunately, the assistant didn't hide the scale number well, and my eyes found it. They practically popped out of my head! I thought she must have written it down wrong.

The next day, I dusted off my scale at home and stepped on it. The number didn't lie; I had gained a significant amount of weight since my last doctor's appointment six months ago.

My mind started reeling. How did this happen?

You might assume this story took place in my twenties. In fact, this was last year.

I am human. You are too. And while I truly believe that we can be healthy at every size and that weight shouldn't be our focus, I'm also acutely aware that diet culture has convinced us that we need to manage the sizes of our bodies.

(Also, if you started here, I'm so glad to meet you, but please go back and read Part One and then come back!)

May I confess something? I really didn't want to include this chapter. I wish we could keep our focus off of the scale, but I'm also aware that this is something many young women are interested in. I'd rather you receive this information in the context of the love, truth, grace, and balance that's in this book than ask Google. Influencer "experts" may give you terrible diet culture advice or lead you to fads that don't have a holistically healthy you in mind. If someone tells you to hit the gym before school, skip breakfast and lunch, and run three miles after school, please... run the other way.

Diet culture wants you to manage your size

Do you remember when we discussed diet culture in Chapter 11? One of the false things diet culture tries to teach us is that thinness and body size is equated with health. It uses food and exercise as a way to manage our God-given body size rather than honoring the God-given body we have.

I don't want you to feel like you need to manage your body size. However, I do want you to figure out how to feel and function well. I will call this *optimizing our original body*. It may result in your body changing; it may not. The goal is to treat the one body God gave you with respect, care, and love.

One reason trying to manage your size is not something I recommend is that weight regain after loss is typical. In fact, in an analysis of twenty-nine long-term weight loss studies, more than half of the loss was regained within two years, and by five years more than 80% of that lost weight was regained.[1]

Tempted to count your calories? As ESPN's Lee Corso says, "*Not so fast.*" The law allows estimates to be off by as much as 20 percent.[2] Tracking numbers on a "calories in, calories out" basis is like trying to count the hairs on your head. Even if you could, you're constantly growing and losing hair. Just like only God knows how many hairs we have on our heads (Luke 12:7), our wise, God-created body intuitively knows how much food we need. Trust it.

How to optimize your original body

Let's think of optimization as a set of stairs. Seven stairs, in fact. They build on each other, so it's important to not skip any.

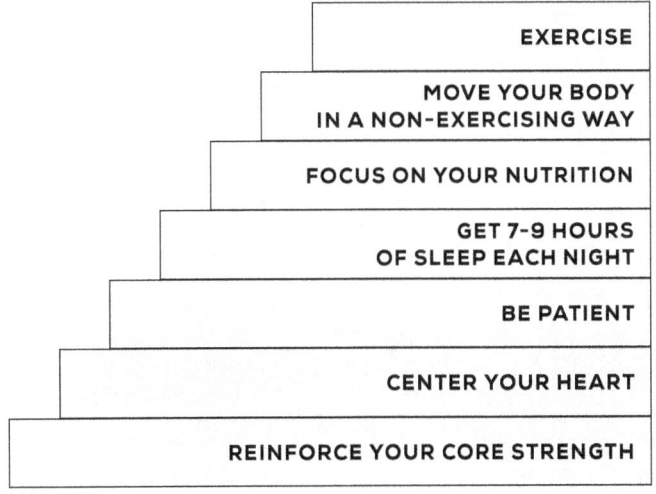

Step 1: Reinforce Your CORE Strength

This first step is critical, and it goes back to the CORE Strength we've discussed throughout the book, especially in Part One: *We take care of our original bodies in a variety of ways so we can do what we are called to do.*

Why?

Diet culture sneaks in so many areas of our lives that it's hard to get away from it. That's why it's important to keep ourselves aligned with what God is calling us to do with our bodies, not with what sizes our bodies are.

Step 2: Center Your Heart

If you want to lose weight, I have a question for you. Please honestly consider your answer: *Why do you want to lose weight?*

Often we have what's called *external motivation* for losing weight: to fit in with our friend group, to gain the interest of that cute science lab partner, to increase our sense of self-worth, or because we think it's something we are supposed to do because that's what society has told us.

God doesn't ask us to be a certain size for any of the reasons listed above. Like we talked about in Chapter 3, body ideals are ever-changing and man-made, not God-designed. In Bible-speak, this is also called "the ways of the world." They are messages our culture sends that don't always line up with God's Word. There are several Bible verses that talk about "the world," but I think this is most appropriate for this chapter:

> See to it that no one takes you captive through hollow and deceptive philosophy, which depends on human tradition and the elemental spiritual forces of this world rather than on Christ. **Colossians 2:8**

In other words, don't be fooled by the diet culture messages you may hear and see about weight. These are deceptive, man-made goals that the enemy has planted to pull our hearts away from Jesus. Center your heart on taking care of your body for your CORE Strength, not for external factors that can fail us.

Step 3: Be Patient

It takes time to create new habits. And I don't mean regular Amazon shipping vs. Prime shipping time. I mean envision the slowest frame rate of a video taken in slo-mo. Your patience in feeling comfortable in these habits should last not just days. Not weeks. Maybe months. Potentially *years*.

Just like pool cannonballs are better in slo-mo, so are health habits. These habits can be anything from relearning to eat when you're hungry and stopping when you're satisfied, getting good sleep, making choices for yourself, staying hydrated, or moving your body. If any of these are new to you, it will take time before they feel natural. Be patient... you'll get there!

Step 4: Get Seven to Nine Hours of Sleep Each Night

Between school, activities, studying, athletics, jobs, youth groups, and family time, this one can be incredibly challenging, but skimping on your sleep can have a negative effect on your goals. Chapter 9 included tips for sleeping better, but what does sleep have to do with the rest of our bodies?

Not getting enough sleep will:

> » **Disrupt the hormones that impact metabolism.** When you don't get enough sleep, this increases ghrelin (the hunger hormone) and decreases leptin (the satiety hormone that says you're full). Studies have also shown that not getting enough sleep can make fat loss harder.[3]
>
> » **Make you crave easy energy.** When you haven't had enough sleep, which restores your energy, your body asks you for quick energy in the form of convenient foods and sugar (See Step 5!).
>
> » **Keep you from thinking clearly.** And if you can't think clearly, you may not make the choices that make you feel and function well in the long run. I've never craved a rainbow of fruits while tired, but I have craved a rainbow of Skittles. Guess which one is easier to grab?

Step 5: Focus on Your Nutrition

After these first few critical steps, what you put in your body will have the most impact on how your body responds.

We've talked about carbohydrates (Chapter 17), fiber (Chapter 29), sugar (Chapter 18), fat (Chapter 16), and protein (Chapter 15). Go back and refresh if it's been a minute since you've read about the importance of those things.

I know I sound like a broken record, but it's worth saying for a final time: I do not believe there are "good" and "bad" foods (Chapter 10), but there are some foods that make us feel and function better. It's like Paul teaches us in 1 Corinthians 10:23 (NLT): "You say, 'I am allowed to do anything,'— but not everything is good for you. You say, 'I am allowed to do anything'— but not everything is beneficial.'"

Mostly choose foods that are beneficial and that build you up. Start there and see how those foods affect your body. You'll need to become your own research scientist to see what foods are the most impactful on your overall health and function.

Here are my top ten nutrition tips for optimizing your body:

1. **Eat.** Fuel your brain and body. You deserve this. Don't skip meals in an effort to manage your body size. Again: eat.

2. **Choose nutritionally dense foods.** Nutritionally dense foods that have plenty of Mighty Micronutrients and macronutrients provide the variety your brain and body needs to feel and function well (see Chapter 12 for a refresher).

3. **Pay attention.** When you eat, pay attention to the flavors and textures of the food you're consuming. Enjoy the presence of others around you. This is called mindful eating. This will help you chew slower and savor what you eat. It will also increase the satisfaction factor of your meal, helping you to eat what your body needs, but not more.

4. **Set your phone face down and out of arm's reach.** Studies have shown that eating while scrolling social media or

watching YouTube causes you to eat more because you're distracted and not paying attention to your body's signals.[4]

5. **Eat breakfast.** Your body and brain need energy for the day. Don't forget that I have single-serve recipes in the Resource Guide that can be enjoyed as breakfast.

6. **Choose high-fiber foods.** Foods like fruits, vegetables, whole grains, and beans will fill you up and help flush you out.

7. **Consume adequate protein.** Typically, this looks like having a serving of protein the size of the palm of your hand with each meal (or three to four times a day). See Chapter 15 if you need a refresher on quality protein sources.

8. **Pair a carb with protein and fat.** If/when you snack, eat at least two of the three macronutrients to balance your blood sugar. Pair a banana and peanut butter, an apple and string cheese, pistachios and coconut milk, or plain Greek yogurt topped with berries and granola.

9. **Choose fruit instead of sugary snacks** to get some extra Mighty Micronutrients.

10. **Limit the calories you drink (except dairy).** Sodas, slushies, and Starbucks are often full of more sugar and energy (or calories) than we need at once. Alcohol's calories are "empty," meaning there is no value in the calories, so avoid this as well.

I can't give you a specific formula for these because God made each of our bodies uniquely with different needs. Your daily activity level will also guide how much you need. If you have specific nutrition needs or questions, I highly recommend speaking with a registered dietitian. You can ask around for recommendations or search the pro finder at IntuitiveEating.org.

Step 6: Move Your Amazing Body in a Non-Exercising Way

When you walk downstairs to tell your parent something rather than texting them, play tug with your dog, or enjoy spikeball with your friends, you are participating in what is called NEAT (non-exercise activity thermogenesis). I do this by taking short walks with my dog throughout the day and keeping my office printer in a different room than my office. It always feels good to get up and move around after sitting for a while.

Having a high NEAT is one of the lifestyle habits identified in people who live in Blue Zones, which are areas with high concentrations of people who reach age 100.[5] Moving naturally is one way we can honor all our body can do. There's nothing wrong with a Netflix binge, but consider balancing that out with some natural movement. When we do this, we are using our bodies in a way that supports doing whatever God is asking us to do for the day.

Step 7: Exercise

Are you surprised to see this last? No amount of exercise can make up for eating more than we need to and not getting enough sleep. Besides, you won't get the training benefits you want without taking the other steps first.

We've talked a lot about exercise, but in a nutshell, here are my recommendations if you're trying to optimize your body:

» Strength training two to three times per week, with at least forty-eight hours in between strength training sessions

» High Intensity Interval Training (HIIT) one to two times per week

» Low to moderate exercise like walking, bike riding, or mind-body work like yoga, Tai Chi, or B.COMPLETE one to two times per week

If exercising is new to you, take the time to ramp up to this recommendation (slo-mo progress, remember?)

While it's helpful and beneficial to get into an exercise rhythm, it's also important to know that your health will not be negatively impacted if you miss a workout.

One more important thing...

Before we wrap up this chapter, I want to remind you of the set point theory we discussed in Chapter 7. Your body has a natural size where it wants to stay. Again, this is God-designed.

If you are utilizing this stair-step technique to change your body size, it may be that it doesn't change much. If that's the case, listen closely: *you've done nothing wrong.* What you think you should look like and what your body wants to naturally be may be two different things.

This is where I ended up after discovering my recent weight gain. My doctor wasn't a bit concerned, because all the factors we discussed in Chapter 7 were totally fine. Additionally, it's not unusual for body size to change in the life stage I'm in. I'm finally to the point where how I feel and function is more important than the number on the scale.

Rather than focusing on your weight, I'd rather you focus on how you feel and function (stay tuned for Chapter 31!). Together, we can ditch diet culture and gain confidence in our God-created original bodies.

But don't let this peaceful summary fool you: I have to revisit my CORE Strength just as much as I'm recommending it to you. But I have faith in us; we can do hard things!

Part Three

COOL DOWN

Phew! That was a lot. Do you feel like you just ran through an intense circuit workout, going from one thing to another? I do.

I have so much more I want to tell you, but that would just be too much. After we cool down, I'll share some other ways I'll be answering your questions.

Do you remember how I said I view the cool-down as a way to put the body back together? In this cool-down, I want to address a few more things to get our whole selves back together. We'll be considering some final mindset strategies surrounding health and our bodies, and I want you to feel "put together" by the time we finish up.

Turn down the volume, lower the lights, and let's cool down with some gentleness and grace.

Chapter 31

HOW DO I KNOW IF I'M SUCCESSFUL AT BEING HEALTHY?

A friend of mine sent me a text that echoed the frustrations of so many clients and friends I've heard from over the years. She'd been taking better care of herself for a few months, getting up early to exercise, and changing her eating habits. After six weeks, the number on her scale hadn't budged.

She wrote, "I'm working my literal butt off, and my head is beginning to tell my heart this isn't working because it's taking forever."

We had a long text conversation as I tried to shift her mindset from defining success by the number on the scale to identifying other benefits.

Don't let your perception of success hinge on a number. Instead, honestly assess other areas of your life that may be seeing improvements.

If you've gotten this far with me, these two questions to help define your success will not surprise you:

Don't let your perception of success hinge on a number.

1. Do I feel better?

Admittedly, this is fairly subjective, but you might notice that you have:

- » More energy to do your daily micro callings
- » Increased immunity (and you're getting sick less often)
- » Fewer mood swings (with the grace to acknowledge that PMS can really do a number on us)
- » Increased confidence in your decision-making and what you are able to do
- » Enhanced mental well-being
- » Less stress and shame about what you eat

2. Do I function better?

In time, you may notice some of these ways you go about your day better:

- » You're physically stronger
- » You get less winded
- » Your general fitness or athletic performance has improved
- » You don't have midafternoon crashes
- » You sleep better and feel more rested in the morning
- » Your poops are better (do not underestimate how important good poops are!)

I've specifically not listed things like weight or size because does that really, truly matter? I don't think it does.

This is going to sound morbid, but imagine yourself in your last days on earth. Are you going to wish you had spent your time and energy trying to weigh five, ten, or twenty pounds less? Or are you going to wish you'd cherished the body you were in and did things you love doing with people you love?

I cannot stress enough the benefits of feeling and functioning well. You probably define that differently than I do. After all, our life stages and goals are different. But that is what will enable us to do what God is calling us to do today and in the future.

Drop the scale when defining success and pick up on how you feel and function. THAT is true success!

Chapter 32

A QUICK NOTE ABOUT YOUR MOM FROM A MOM

Author's note: *While this chapter uses the word "mom," it's applicable to any person who cares about you. Families show up in different ways, so if "mom" isn't applicable to you, replace it in your head with the appropriate person.*

A friend of mine was attending a black tie event with a coworker, who we will call Emma. Emma's parents happened to live nearby, so she got ready at her parents' house to make it easier for my friend to pick her up. When Emma got in the car, my friend piled on the compliments.

"Emma, you look stunning! That color is amazing on you, and your dress fits like a glove. Just so beautiful! I bet your mom couldn't stop talking about how wonderful you look!"

Emma shook her head. "She didn't. Actually, she has never made a comment about how I look, good or bad."

"Never?"

"Not. Once," she sighed.

We've probably heard of (and possibly experienced) parents or other loved ones making negative comments about our food choices or bodies. We may be familiar with parents who layer on so many positive compliments that it feels fake and has lost its impact. And now I hear this story, of a parent's silence causing pain.

This is one chapter with no question, but a message I desperately want you to know.

Lean in, my friend. This is important. This is something that took me years to know and even longer to truly understand—until I became a parent.

This is the secret most moms carry:

We have no idea what we are doing.

I mean, sure, maybe your mom can get her whiteboard out and schedule a summer calendar like no one can. Maybe she can run a conference call one minute and root you on from the sidelines the next. Maybe she can take the red-eye home from a business meeting and still get you to school on time.

But when it comes to raising daughters with a healthy body image, most moms are terrified. Why? Because thanks to diet culture, many of us have had our own body image issues our whole lives and don't want to pass them down to our daughters. In countless conversations

I've had with other grown women, I can count how many grew up with a positive body image: two. *Two!*

We are trying. Many of us are learning new ways of fostering our relationships with food and our bodies in the midst of raising our children. Much of what you've read in this book is a new mindset I've developed over the last ten years while raising my own children.

I remember being in middle school, trying on clothes in the Macy's fitting room. As I pulled the curtain to get some privacy, I noticed a tall, slim girl about my age going into a different fitting room. Because my body was still changing and because clothing sizes can vary so much, I needed a few different sizes for the items I'd chosen.

When my mom yelled out, "Do you need me to get a bigger size?" I was horrified and snapped back with a not-so-nice "no," even though I did.

The story I had made up in my head was that this tall, slender girl would think less of me because I had to get a bigger size. The fact that I had no idea who she was didn't matter in my fourteen-year-old mind. The story in my head wasn't real, but my feelings were.

My mom was trying to help, but had no idea how vulnerable I felt.

While reading this book, you may start to identify words or phrases that make you feel vulnerable with your loved ones. Maybe you've started adjusting your mindset about how you think about health. (If so, I am jumping up and down and cheering you on!) But maybe those aren't aligned with things you hear often from the people you care about.

Here are some responses to consider if you're feeling hurt by the words people say to you:

- » **Make a Boundary Sandwich** like we discussed in Chapter 5. Not sure what to say? I'll get you started:

    "(Name), I know you care about me. But when you make comments about _____, it makes me feel like I'm not good enough. I don't believe that's how you feel, so I'd appreciate it if you didn't make comments about _____ anymore."

- » **Ask kind and curious questions**, like:
    - Did you ever have body image issues growing up?
    - What do you wish you could change about your relationship with food?
    - What is something you struggled with as a young adult that you wish you could change?

    Then truly listen. You may learn something new about your mom.

- » **Together, visit a counselor or registered dietitian** certified in intuitive eating. Find one by searching the counselor directory at IntuitiveEating.org.

If I were to guess, Emma's mom was so scared of saying something wrong that she didn't say anything at all. I understand that fear and empathize with her. But silence can still hurt. So do small comments, and big ones too. Even a three-second comment can send us down a three-year spiral in our heads. We all have the capability of hurting or helping someone with our tongues, and sometimes those tongues hurt others without knowing it.

If possible, give your mom some grace. And if something said (or unsaid) hurts, speak up. Point her to the Parents' Guide I created (link in the Resource Guide). If you can't say something to her, a counselor can help you navigate those feelings.

Chapter 33

HOW DO I BREAK FREE FROM COMPARISON?

Sometimes I look around and get very, very discouraged.

I'm a personal trainer and nutrition coach, for crying out loud, and yet my body is getting bigger. I know this is because of my age and stage. But instead of having a body that's still developing, like yours is, mine is going through the early stages of menopause and closing up the baby-making shop. I'm fine with not making any more babies (reason number one is that I couldn't handle the sleepless nights anymore), but I'm not as fine with the natural weight gain that comes from hormonal changes.

It's hard not to compare myself to other women my age who haven't struggled with this same body change.

And then I feel the same way I did when I was a teenager, comparing myself to others.

Sadly, I know this continues with young women today. My private conversations and research confirm what I intuitively know:

comparison is worse now than it ever was before. Even if we aren't comparing our bodies, we can compare friendships, grades, money, designer clothes, Instagram followers, and even which phone model we carry.

We can blame a lot of things, including photo app filters, highlight reels, and constant barrages of images of people who may or may not even be real human beings.

When we constantly see images like that, it's like the neural pathways we discussed in Chapter 8: they grow deeper and deeper in our brains until the fake images turn into reality.

But they aren't real. We forget that highlight reels aren't real life. We know this on a logical level, and this probably isn't the first time you've heard it. However, with every scroll and heart and double tap, we fall deeper into thinking the highlight reel is real.

It's not. What *is* real is the original body God created in you. Sometimes we just have to be intentional about remembering that.

Here are three things I do when comparison strikes:
Spot it: *Notice the thoughts of comparison.*

Have you ever had a friend point out something you had in your teeth? (When they do this kindly, these are wonderful friends. Please do the same for me.) You can't do anything about that strawberry seed in between your front teeth if you don't know about it. Similarly, you can't conquer your comparison-spiral thoughts unless you stop and intentionally notice them as they're happening. Take note when you start to compare yourself to others.

Lock it: *Imagine throwing that thought in a prison cell.*

Comparison violates my boundary of being kind to myself. (You should have that boundary as well... no Inner Mean Girl, remember?) Paul calls this taking your thoughts captive in 2 Corinthians 10:5:

> We demolish arguments and every pretension that sets itself up against the knowledge of God, and we take captive every thought to make it obedient to Christ.

Take your thought captive and throw it in a prison cell.

> **Pro Tip:** *Consider locking out and unfollowing social media accounts that focus on diet culture and instead follow accounts that promote peace and freedom in our food and bodies. You can find a list of recommended Instagram accounts in the Resource Guide.*

Speak it: *Have a positive phrase ready that you can speak back to yourself.*

Mine is, "I'm taking care of myself so I can do what I'm called to do." You can borrow that or make up your own. Play around with these:

» God created my original body with and for an original purpose.

- » If I was her, I wouldn't be me. And I like me.
- » Her outside doesn't tell the story on the inside.
- » Her path is not my path ... and God knows where I'm going.

That's it. Simple, right?

Simple, but not easy.

If they are honest, most grown women will admit to having issues with comparison. How do I know this? From conversations, but also from statistics. Approximately 91% of women are unhappy with their bodies.[1] I blame comparison.

One of the reasons I wrote this book was to break the cycle of comparison and poor body image ... or at least put a little crack in it and let you shake it until it breaks. It's something I wish I'd had when I was younger. Thoughts of comparison and what my body looked like held way too much space in my brain for too long.

You deserve better. So much better.

Creating the habit now of squelching the comparison monster will keep it from taking up space for the rest of your life. It is one of the best ways of being kind to yourself, both now and in the future.

Chapter 34

I FEEL AND FUNCTION WELL. IS THAT IT?

"I just wish there was a pill I could take that would make me healthy." —*Me, for way too much of my life*

How about you? Have you ever thought this? If so, you're not alone. The ease of it would certainly be nice.

While there's not a magic health pill, my hope is that I've empowered you throughout this book with knowledge and wisdom about how to have a healthy relationship with food, movement, and your body.

I can't responsibly let you go, though, without this truth:

Even with a body that feels and functions well, life's challenges won't fade.

- » Six-pack abs don't prevent hurting hearts.
- » Eating your vegetables won't keep your parents together.

» Losing ten pounds won't get—or keep—a love interest. (And if it does, I caution you about the foundation of that relationship.)

Hard things happen no matter how healthy you are or what you look like.

Taking care of yourself is not a magical bubble of protection. Bad things happen to healthy people. Yes, we have research touting the benefits of exercise and eating well. It's all true. But it's not a guarantee. All the almonds, spinach, and workouts in the world don't prevent heartache. Our friendships change. Parents get divorced. We don't get accepted to our dream schools. We find ourselves in a global pandemic.

That's why my relationship with Jesus is the foundation of all I do... even more than having the foundation of a strong CORE.

Jesus told us to expect hard times in John 16:33: "In this world you *will* have trouble. But take heart! I have overcome the world" (emphasis mine).

We *will* have trouble. Putting my faith and trust in Jesus doesn't prevent hard times, but it does help me get through them.

And here's the best part—we don't have to earn Jesus's love, forgiveness, or grace. We just get those things by inviting Him into our hearts.

Just like I'm not asking you to abide by a bunch of rules to take care of yourself, Jesus isn't asking you to follow a bunch of rules to follow Him.

If you don't have a relationship with Jesus, consider it. You can offer a simple prayer like this:

> *"Jesus, I know I've messed up. I'm not perfect. But I know you came to cover all the times I've messed up so I can live with You in heaven. Please come into my heart and guide me in my thoughts and ways."*

Then get to know Him by talking to Him through prayer and reading God's Word in the Bible. I said it earlier, but the book of John is a good place to start. You can also download a Bible app. There you'll find plans, short videos, and guided prayers to help you grow your relationship.

It really is that easy. Even a "healthy pill" can't compare to what Jesus can do for you.

Chapter 35

CONCLUSION

Each year in January, gyms across the country watch their weight rooms and fitness centers fill up. I also saw this when I led classes at fitness centers. Our social media feeds also fill up with weight loss ads making promises they can't keep.

Three weeks later, it's easier to find a parking space at the gym and use the equipment. Research shows that by the end of January, 43% of people have given up on their New Year's resolutions and only 9% actually stick with them.[1] Not surprisingly, the top three resolutions are to exercise more, eat healthier, and lose weight.[2]

If you close this book ready to make big and fast changes in your eating and exercising, I applaud the intent. But I also beg you: **slow down**.

What? Why?

Because I don't want you to treat taking care of yourself like a New Year's resolution. My hope and prayer is that this book has given you a new mindset about why you take care of yourself. If you have new tactics you want to try as a result of this, here is my advice: **start small.**

Pick one small thing you want to change, like:

- » Putting your phone down an hour before bedtime
- » Drinking an extra glass of water
- » Eating an extra plant each day
- » Connecting with God outside for five minutes each day

Once you're used to doing that, add something else. These small actions will lead to big results over time.

My hope in writing this book is that I've helped you change your relationship with your food, exercise, and body. And the best way to do that is with small steps. Baby steps, if you will.

As I've gone through the process of writing this book, I've often used the shorthand YCS for Your CORE Strength. I have YCS notes on my phone, in my planner, and on my calendar. When inspiration hits, if I don't jot it down, I won't remember it. I've gotten good at making one-handed notes while brushing my teeth with the other hand, and my neighbors have likely seen me voice typing while on a walk. All are #YCS.

I hope and pray that YCS plays a part in your life in some way, whether it's empowering you to choose the foods that make you feel good, moving your body in new ways, or embracing a new mindset about taking care of yourself.

We've covered so much in these pages. If I were to choose three things for you to remember using my YCS acronym, it would be these:

You are an originally designed work of art made by God, created to live out a purpose He has for you.

Choose to take care of yourself in a way that works for you.

Strength is displayed not only in your muscles, but also in your mental health, mindset, and meaningful relationships with God and others.

Now, take those three words and put them together:

You choose strength.

In these pages, I hope you've discovered a new definition of strength, and especially CORE Strength.

Tears are welling up in my eyes as I envision a new you—not in the physical sense, but with a transformed mind. One who is:

- » Strong in the knowledge of how to take care of yourself holistically
- » Self-assured in the original body God gave you
- » Secure in God's abundant love of and purpose for you

Be warned: it will be hard to stay strong in your CORE Strength. After all, we have an enormous industry full of money and influencers that want to sell you a diet culture promise they can't keep. But we aren't here to chase after the world's promises. We are here to fulfill God's purpose for us. The words of Paul in his letter to the Romans come to mind:

> Do not conform to the pattern of this world, but be transformed by the renewing of your mind. Then you will be able to test and approve what God's will is—his good, pleasing and perfect will. **Romans 12:2**

Finally, I leave you with the same words I say on my *Graced Health* podcast, which are definitely not the ways of the world, but, I do believe, in line with God's will for us:

Your eating, movement and body don't have to be perfect. You just need to be able to do what you're called to do.

I'm rooting for you, and I care so deeply for you. You are strong, my friend. Be well.

WHAT'S NEXT?

I have so enjoyed this journey with you. I hope you have as well. Can we stay connected?

Head over to GracedHealth.com/Your-CORE-Strength. There, I have free downloads and links to other products I've made to support this journey. This is also where you'll find the discussion guide I mentioned in Chapter 4.

I've also created a Parents' Guide to Your CORE Strength. This is a summary of what we discussed in these pages. You can tell your parents it's like the Cliff Notes version (they'll know what it means). It may also be helpful if they ask you questions about your new mindset and approach to wellness. You can also find this at GracedHealth.com/Your-CORE-Strength.

We can also stay connected through your ears! My new podcast, *Lessons to My Teenage Self*, is just that. I created it specifically for you, and it will share additional lessons I wish I knew when I was younger — plus, I'll be bringing in other young adults to share what they've learned. We'll also have various experts to help you continue taking care of your physical, mental, and spiritual health. Find *Lessons to My Teenage Self* on your favorite podcast platform as well as on YouTube.

If this book was valuable to you, can you do two free, but highly valuable, things for me?

1. **Leave a review on Amazon.** Share with another potential reader what you liked or how this book helped you. Even just two sentences is meaningful!

2. **Share this book** with a friend, coach, or youth director. Word-of-mouth referrals are the very best way to reach others. (Better yet, post on the social of your choice using #yourcorestrength.)

I'm so grateful for you. Thank you!

Your CORE Strength Resources

RESOURCE GUIDE

As promised, here are the workouts, recipes, and other resources I mentioned throughout the book. Enjoy!

HELPFUL ORGANIZATIONS

» NEDA.org

The National Eating Disorders Association (NEDA) is the largest nonprofit organization dedicated to supporting individuals and families affected by eating disorders. NEDA supports individuals and families affected by eating disorders and serves as a catalyst for prevention, cures, and access to quality care.

» EatRight.org

The Academy of Nutrition and Dietetics offers information on nutrition and health, from meal planning and prep to choices that can help prevent or manage health conditions and more. You can also search for a Registered Dietitian on this site.

» IntuitiveEating.org

Intuitive Eating is a self-care eating framework that integrates instinct, emotion, and rational thought and was created by two dietitians, Evelyn Tribole and Elyse Resch, in 1995. Intuitive Eating is a weight-inclusive, evidence-based model with a validated assessment scale and over one hundred studies to date. You can search for a certified Intuitive Eating Counselor on this site.

- » PsychologyToday.com

    Find a therapist or search the comprehensive list of articles supporting your mental health.

- » FaithfulCounseling.com

    Connect with a fellow believer online within their network of licensed, professional therapists.

- » BetterHelp.com

    Making professional therapy accessible, affordable, and convenient—so anyone who struggles with life's challenges can get help, anytime and anywhere.

INSTAGRAM ACCOUNTS TO CHECK OUT

These are useful accounts to follow to continue learning how to fuel, move, and gain confidence in your body without diet culture. I may not agree with every single word or idea these accounts have shared (or will share), but I do find their content generally useful, helpful, and uplifting.

- Amy Connell, Lessons to My Teenage Self Podcast (@lessons.pod)
- Amy Connell, Graced Health (@gracedhealth)
- Amanda Coates Reynolds (@thewellway_amanda)
- Amanda Martinez Beck, Author (@your_body_is_good)
- Anna Marie Long Nutrition (@annamarie.rd)
- Body BLoved (@body_bloved)
- Brittany Braswell, Food Freedom & Body Image Coach for Christian Women (@brittanybraswellrd)
- Brittany Wilson (@brittanywilsonrdn)
- Char-Lee Cassel, MS, RDN, CEP (@charlee.cassel)
- Christyna, MS, RDN, LDN (@encouragingdietitian)
- Dr. Kari Anderson (@myeatingdoctor)
- FINDINGbalance (@findingbalanceofficial)
- Heather Creekmore, Body Image Freedom (@comparedtowho)

- Intuitive Eating Podcast (@intuitive.eating.podcast)
- Joyful Health Co (@joyfulhealthco)
- Kasey Shuler (@kaseybshuler)
- Kristen Bunger, RD, Non-Diet Nutritionist (@kristenbunger.rd)
- Kristin Williams (@wonderfullymadenutrition)
- Leslie Schilling (@leslieschilling)
- Liesel Maddox (@dietitian.liesel)
- Megan Becker, Christian Dietitian & Health Coach (@gracerootednutrition)
- Megan Hadley MS, RDN, LDN (@meg.hadley)
- Rock Recovery (@rockrecovery)
- Tracy Brown, Dietitian (@tracybrownrd)
- Victoria Yates, RN-BSN and Intuitive Eating & Body Image Coach (@nondiet_rn)

BOOKS

» *Your New Playlist: The Student's Guide to Tapping into the Superpower of Mindset* by Jon Acuff and his daughters L. E. and McRae

» *Wonderfully Made: Discover the Identify, Love, and Worth You Were Created For* by Allie Marie Smith

» *Killing Comparison: Reject the Lie You Aren't Good Enough and Live Confident in Who God Made You to Be* by Nona Jones

» *Feed Yourself: Step Away from the Lies of Diet Culture and into Your Divine Design* by Leslie Schilling

» *The Intuitive Eating Workbook for Teens: a Non-Diet, Body Positive Approach to Building a Healthy Relationship with Food* by Elyse Resch

» *Your Worthy Body: Find Freedom in Health by Breaking All the Rules* by (me!) Amy Connell

PODCASTS

» *Lessons to My Teenage Self* by (me!) **Amy Connell**

I've created this new podcast especially for you! Learn what I wish I'd known as a teen about taking care of my physical, mental, and spiritual health. With a mix of solo and guest podcasts, you'll hear more Pro Tips and applicable ways of optimizing your wellness right now so you don't have to figure them out later! Listen on your favorite podcast app or watch on YouTube.

» *The Joy-Filled Eater* by **Brittany Braswell, RD**

A no-fluff food, freedom, and body image podcast for Christian women. Brittany spills the tea on all things diet culture and helps you cultivate a joy-filled relationship with food, your body, and Jesus.

» *Compared to Who?* by **Heather Creekmore**

Are you looking for biblical encouragement for your body image and comparison issues? Look no further than the *Compared to Who?* show! Each week you'll hear encouragement, biblical truth, and practical strategies to help you fight and win your battles with insecurity, body shame, constant comparison, and approval.

» *The Old School Food Freedom Podcast* by Chrissy Kirkman

Join FINDING*balance* executive director Chrissy Kirkman as she interviews a wide range of biblically sound experts, thought leaders, artists, and everyday people who will inspire you to interrupt negative cultural soundtracks and get back to the old-school basics of God's original design for our relationship with food and our bodies.

» *The Move Your Body Differently Podcast* by Shaela Daugherty.

Learn how your theology of God impacts your wellness journey! This podcast is for you if you are working toward a healthy and fit lifestyle and need both spiritual and mental encouragement for the journey.

» *The Joyful Health Show* by Kasey Shuler

Cut through the weeds of wellness rules and learn to trust God's good design for your body. Discover joyful health by grace: intuitive eating, joyful movement, embodiment, and mental well-being for Christians.

» *The Huberman Lab* by Dr. Andrew Huberman

The Huberman Lab is a podcast by Dr. Andrew Huberman, a neuroscientist and tenured professor in the department of neurobiology and, by courtesy, psychiatry and behavioral sciences at Stanford School of Medicine.

He has a passion for providing research-based topics on wellness at zero cost to the consumer. I appreciate that he presents facts and findings with no bias and encourages listeners to apply what works for them.

While his podcasts are lengthy and heavily science-focused (sometimes I don't get all the chemistry he shares), they are worth the listen. This is not a faith-based show.

These are three episodes I especially recommend:

- "What Alcohol Does to Your Body, Brain & Health" (August 22, 2022)
- "The Effects of Cannabis (Marijuana) on the Brain & Body" (October 2, 2022)

Pro Tip: *The last forty-five minutes or so of this show, beginning around the 2:18:00 mark, specifically applies to the adolescent brain and body. Feel free to skip ahead.*

- "Sleep Toolkit: Tools for Optimizing Sleep & Sleep-Wake Timing" (August 8, 2022)

Pro Tip: *If you search for these episodes at HubermanLab.com, you'll find time stamps where you can skip to the content you're specifically interested in.*

WORKOUTS

» **B.COMPLETE: The ultimate low-impact complement to however you like to move your body**

B.COMPLETE is my signature online, on-demand class that can be used as an active recovery day, as a low-impact workout, or to "pre-hab" your body. Buy it once and do it as many times as you want!

Find more information at GracedHealth.com/B-COMPLETE or GracedHealth.com/Your-CORE-Strength.

» **YouTube**

Check out these YouTube videos referenced throughout the workout chapters:

Warmup

5 Favorite Core Exercises

10-Minute Core Workout

Foam Rolling

YOUR CORE STRENGTH

6 Types of Functional Movements

Types of Stretching

Mini Muscles

Bodyweight Workout

Pulling Exercises (bands)

Pulling Exercises (loops)

Cooldown

B.COMPLETE

FUNCTIONAL MOVEMENTS

These are movements that fall in the "functional movement" category. This is not a comprehensive list! I tried to choose exercises that are adequately executed through your own body weight or through resistance bands. If you have other forms of resistance (e.g., dumbbells), then by all means use those.

 You may find demos to all of these in the "Movement Demos" Playlist on my YouTube channel.

Push
1. Lying band chest press
2. Push-ups
3. Band flye
4. Standing band chest press

Squat
1. Squat
2. Plie squat
3. Goblet squat
4. Sumo squat

Lunge/Single Leg
1. Single-leg sit to stand
2. Single-leg squat with reach
3. Lateral lunge

Pull
1. Bent-over row
2. Band pull down
3. Reverse fly
4. Prone band lateral extension pulls

Hinge
1. Deadlifts
2. Single-leg deadlifts
3. Good mornings
4. Kettlebell swings

Rotational
1. Diagonal lunge
2. High-to-low band chop
3. Low-to-high band chop
4. Bicycles

To plan a workout, choose one of these combinations:

- » Push and Pull
- » Squat and Hinge
- » Lunge/Single-Leg and Rotational

Perform alternating numbers in each combination (1, 1, 2, 2, 3, 3, etc.). For example, in a push/pull workout, do lying band chest press, bent-over row, push-ups, band pull down, etc. Do each movement eight times, working your way up to twenty reps, before moving on to the next movement.

For more intensity, focus on only one combination, and repeat the round for a total of two to five times. For less intensity, go through all three combinations.

RECIPES

Amy's Top Five Kitchen Pro Tips

1. If you have long hair, tie it back while you work so you aren't greeted with a stray hair in your mouth later. Ew.

2. Prep and cooking times don't include cleanup. Be sure to clean up after your creation.

3. Try a recipe as it is written once, then adjust it to your liking.

4. Plan ahead! If you know you want to try something, write down the ingredients and ask the grocery shopper in your house to get them the next time they go to the store.

5. The more time you spend in the kitchen, the more comfortable you'll get. It's just like trying a new sport or exercise. At first it's weird, but you'll get used to it. You'll probably have some fails, just like I did (oh, the stories I could tell). Keep trying and learn from your mistakes.

Breakfast Cookie Bowl

Prep: less than five minutes

One morning, we were out of breakfast cookies (you'll see the recipe for those later), and I was trying to help my son come up with an alternative. When I said we could make breakfast cookies and put them in a bowl, he thought that sounded great, and now he does this on his own. Let's be honest — this is basically oatmeal. Whatever you call it, it's a quick way to feed yourself in the morning!

The oats offer complex carbs and lots of fiber while the flax seeds provide some additional fiber as well as Omega-3s for your heart and mental health. The protein and fat in the nut butter will help slow digestion and increase absorption to help keep your belly full until lunch.

Ingredients

- ½ cup rolled oats (gluten-free if necessary)
- 1 Tbsp cocoa powder
- 1 Tbsp ground flax seeds
- 1 Tbsp creamy peanut butter
- 1 Tbsp honey
- ¼ cup warm water (more or less to taste)

Instructions

Mix oats, cocoa powder, and flax seeds in a bowl. Next, add in peanut butter, honey, and warm water to the bowl. (Use more or less water to your preference. I like my oats somewhat chewy, so I use less.) Stir well and enjoy immediately.

Overnight Oats

Prep: less than five minutes
Ready in thirty minutes to several hours

Oats have a reputation for "sticking to your ribs," which isn't really a thing, but they do stay with you a while. I'll make this the night before so I don't have to think or work in the morning while my body and brain are still waking up.

As with the breakfast cookie bowl, adjust the amount of milk to your preference. Use slightly less milk for thicker oats, or slightly more for thinner oats.

> **Pro Tip:** *Frozen berries work well in this, and they relieve you of having to keep fresh fruit on hand all the time.*

> **Pro Tip:** *If bananas are your fruit of choice, they are best cut right before you eat them so they don't brown.*

Ingredients

- ½ cup rolled oats (gluten-free if necessary)
- 1 Tbsp chia seeds
- 1 tsp cinnamon
- 1 cup milk of your choice (dairy or non-dairy)
- ½ cup fruit of your choice (blueberries, strawberries, and mango are my favorites)

Instructions

Combine oats, chia seeds, and cinnamon in a two-cup or larger Mason jar. Stir to mix, then add milk and stir again. Place the fruit on top, then secure with a lid (clear plastic wrap or foil will also work).

Store in the refrigerator for at least thirty minutes or overnight. Stir and enjoy.

> **Pro Tip:** *If you're using frozen fruit and only letting the oats set for thirty minutes, thaw the fruit for thirty-five to forty seconds in the microwave before adding.*

Egg Sandwich

Prep: less than five minutes

Like a savory breakfast? Throw this together to eat before school or even on the go.

Ingredients

- » 1 whole wheat English muffin, sliced lengthwise in half
- » 1 egg
- » 1 slice of cheese, your choice (my favorite is Swiss; my kids like American)

Optional:

- » 1 slice Canadian bacon or 2 slices regular bacon (I like the pre-cooked bacon, or you can use leftovers)

Instructions

Toast English muffin on medium setting in toaster or toaster oven.

While muffin is in the toaster, spray a small, shallow bowl with non-stick spray (like Pam). Crack egg into bowl, then gently whisk with a fork. Place the bowl in the microwave with a paper towel over it to prevent a potential explosion (trust me: don't skip the paper towel). Cook for about fifty seconds on power level five or six. Since microwaves are all a bit different and altitude impacts cook time, check to make sure the egg is completely done (you should see no runny whites). If necessary, cook an additional few seconds, making sure to cover with a paper towel each time. Season egg with salt and/or pepper if desired.

When the English muffin is done toasting, layer the bottom half of the muffin, egg, cheese, and top layer of the muffin. If adding the optional Canadian bacon or regular bacon, heat according to package directions (or reheat for a few seconds in the microwave if it's left over) and add between eggs and cheese.

Chia Pudding

Prep: less than five minutes
Ready in two hours

Chia seeds offer a ton of fiber and Omega-3s, and making them with any kind of fortified milk will also help you get your calcium.

You can dress up your chia pudding in a million ways. I've included two ways here that are well-liked at my house, but experiment with what you like. The most important thing is to get the basic ratio right; then you can play around from there.

Ingredients

- 2 Tbsp Chia seeds
- 1 cup milk of your choice
  (I call this the basic ratio)

Instructions

Combine chia seeds and milk in a Mason jar. Shake to combine and place in the refrigerator for two hours. If time allows, give it an extra shake about five minutes after you make it so the chia seeds don't sink to the bottom.

Add-Ins:

Chunky Monkey: 1 Tbsp cocoa powder, ½ mashed banana, ½ tsp cinnamon, 1 tsp honey (combine all with Basic Ratio)

Costa Rica Parfait: After seeds have set, add 1–2 Tbsp granola, ½ cup tropical fruit like mango or frozen mix of strawberry, papaya, and mango, and 1–2 Tbsp shredded coconut

Pro Tip: *Throw together the basic ratio before school and it will be ready for you when you get home from school.*

Pro Tip: *If you wear braces, you may find that chia seeds get stuck in the brackets. Enjoy this snack when you can brush your teeth afterwards, or just pocket this recipe for when you're done with braces.*

Avocado Toast

Prep: about five minutes

When I'm low on magnesium and my muscles are twitchy, this is my go-to remedy. Avocados are high in magnesium, and when I make this with a whole-grain bread like Ezekiel brand, I get a little extra magnesium as well.

Ingredients

- » 1 slice bread (I like Ezekiel whole wheat for the extra fiber and protein)
- » ½ medium avocado
- » Salt, to taste
- » Optional: crushed red pepper, drizzle of honey

Instructions

Toast the bread on a medium setting.

While bread is in the toaster, place the avocado on a cutting board on its side. With a sharp knife, carefully cut down until you feel the pit. Turn the avocado on its side, then spin it around so you are cutting through the full avocado. Place the knife down safely, then twist the two halves of the avocado until they come apart.

> **Pro Tip:** *If you're not familiar with how to cut an avocado, check out the directions at EvolvingTable.com and search "how to cut an avocado."*

Scoop one of the avocado halves into a small bowl, then smash with the backside of a fork.

After bread is done toasting, spread smashed avocado on toast, then add salt to taste. If desired, lightly sprinkle with crusted red pepper and sprinkle with honey.

To add a bit of protein, add a fried egg (see fried egg recipe).

Fried Egg

Prep: about five minutes

I could eat fried eggs every day for almost every meal (until I get tired of them). Eggs are a wonderful source of protein; vitamins like B12, D, A, E, and K; choline for brain development; and lutein for eye health. Plus they are versatile and affordable!

Honestly, you can slap a fried egg on just about anything: toast, a turkey burger, a tortilla, or even a grilled chicken sandwich (see the Big Ames Special later).

It takes about five minutes to make, which is how long it takes to toast a piece of bread. In five minutes, you can enjoy a meal full of protein, carbs, and healthy fat. Win!

Ingredients

- » 1 or 2 large eggs (or more, but I typically fry in groups of no more than 3 because it gets hard to manage in the pan)
- » 2-3 tsp butter
- » Salt and pepper, to taste

Instructions

Choose a 10" nonstick cooking pan. Put it on the stove and turn the heat to medium-low.

> **Pro Tip:** *If you are using a gas range, always make sure the flame isn't lipping up around the pan.*

Add butter to the pan. Allow it to melt and coat the bottom of the pan evenly. Swirl the pan around to make sure the fat covers the surface.

Crack the egg into a small bowl or cup. This makes it easier to add to the pan without getting any eggshells in it.

Gently slide the egg from the bowl or cup into the heated pan.

Sprinkle a pinch of salt and pepper over the egg if you like. You can skip this step if you prefer your egg plain.

Let the egg cook undisturbed for a few minutes until the egg white is set and the yolk is still runny. Gently flip the egg with a spatula and cook for an additional thirty seconds to two minutes. The more well done you like your yolk (the yellow part), the longer you should let it cook after flipping. While it's important that the white is fully cooked, you can play around with the yolk's doneness.

Use a spatula to remove the egg from the pan and place it on your plate.

> **Pro Tip:** *Remember, practice makes perfect, so don't be discouraged if your first attempt isn't perfect. Frying eggs (and cooking in general) is a skill that gets better with time and experience.*

Big Ames Special

Prep: about ten minutes
Ready in about fifteen minutes

"Big Ames" is a nickname my boys gave me at some point. One night our schedule was out of whack and dinnertime arrived with no plan. I dug through my refrigerator and put this together for them. It was a huge hit.

Adjust the ingredients to what you have on hand. You may not always have leftover chicken on hand, but if you mention you'd like to try this to the person who makes your meals, they may make an extra breast or thigh.

Ingredients

- 1 bun (Hawaiian-style buns work especially well with this recipe)
- 1 leftover cooked chicken breast or thigh
- 1 slice cheese, your choice
- Chick-fil-A sauce*
- 1 fried egg
- 2 slices pre-cooked bacon

Instructions

First, prepare your bun by spreading Chick-fil-A sauce on the top and bottom.

Choose a nonstick cooking pan. Put it on the stove and turn the heat to medium-low.

---

* Don't have Chick-fil-A sauce? Make a copycat version! Combine 1/4 cup mayo, 1 tsp mustard, 1 Tbsp BBQ sauce, and 1 Tbsp honey. Mix well and store extra in a glass container with a lid in the refrigerator.

While the pan is heating, cook the bacon in the microwave according to the package directions.

Add 2-3 teaspoons of butter or cooking oil to the pan. Allow it to melt and coat the bottom of the pan evenly. Swirl the pan around to make sure the fat covers the surface.

Crack the egg into a small bowl or cup. This makes it easier to add to the pan without getting any eggshells in it.

Gently slide the egg from the bowl or cup into the heated pan.

Let the egg cook undisturbed for a few minutes until the egg white is set and the yolk is still runny.

While egg is cooking, remove bacon from microwave and reheat the chicken breast or thigh in the microwave until warm. Microwaves vary, so start with forty-five seconds on power level six and add more time if necessary.

Gently flip the egg with a spatula and cook for an additional thirty seconds to two minutes.

Get ready to assemble! Place the chicken on the bottom bun, then add bacon. Place fried egg on top of bacon, then add your cheese and the top bun.

Add some fruit or sliced veggies on the side for some extra Mighty Micronutrients, and be sure to grab a napkin. This one can get a bit messy when you eat it!

Sweet Potato Medallions with Nut Butter

Prep: five minutes
Ready in twenty-five minutes

Sweet potatoes are one of my superfoods. Not only do I love their taste and versatility (Mashed! Roasted! Medallions!) but they seem to have a magical effect on my body. They help me perform, recover, and sleep well.

Because mashed and roasted potatoes take a while (and because most of my family members don't share my love of sweet potatoes), I needed to find a single-serve way to eat them. Enter medallions.

I'll enjoy these as a snack or meal alongside a larger serving of protein.

Ingredients

- » 1 small to medium sweet potato
- » 1 Tbsp nut butter (I prefer peanut, but adjust according to your taste)
- » Spray-on olive oil or 1-2 tsp olive oil
- » Nonstick cooking spray

Instructions

Preheat your oven or toaster oven to 400 degrees.

> **Pro Tip:** *If you have a toaster oven, use it for small-scale oven projects like this. It uses less energy and heats up faster.*

Line a baking sheet with aluminum foil and spray with nonstick cooking spray.

Wash the sweet potato by scrubbing the skin well. Pat dry with a towel or paper towel.

On a cutting board, cut off the ends of the sweet potato and discard. Slice the potato into ¼ inch medallions with a sharp knife. (Visualize a really thick potato chip.)

Transfer the medallions to the baking sheet and spray with olive oil, or brush a bit of olive oil on each one. Roast for approximately fifteen to twenty minutes. You'll know they are done when a fork glides easily into one.

When potatoes are done, remove from oven with a hot pad holder, then transfer to a plate using a spatula.

Potatoes are hot, so you may need to wait a few minutes for them to cool down.

Spread a little peanut butter on each medallion. Enjoy!

Roasted Chickpeas

Prep: five minutes
Ready in thirty minutes

Chickpeas are a fantastic source of protein and fiber, and I love the taste! These are a great snack too.

Ingredients

- 1 15-ounce can chickpeas
- 1 Tbsp olive oil
- ½ tsp salt
- ½ tsp your favorite seasoning (my go-to is chili powder or oregano)

Instructions

Preheat your oven to 400 degrees.

Line a baking sheet with aluminum foil.

Rinse chickpeas in a colander to reduce salt and slime. Pat dry well using a paper towel or extra kitchen towel (just be sure to put the towel in the laundry hamper right after so you don't end up drying dishes with it later).

Place the dried chickpeas in a medium mixing bowl. Drizzle with olive oil and sprinkle with seasonings. Toss to coat evenly with oil and seasonings.

Spread the chickpeas in a single layer on the baking sheet. Bake for twenty to thirty minutes, depending on how crispy you like them. The longer you bake them, the crispier they will be.

Remove from oven and enjoy. Save extras in an airtight container — however, they lose their crispiness easily, so sadly, they won't be the same the next day.

> **Pro Tip:** *Want a healthy treat for your pup? Give your dog a couple of chickpeas. Mine loves them raw!*

KIND TO YOUR FUTURE SELF RECIPES:

*Make-Ahead Multi-Serving Recipes
You Can Enjoy Throughout the Week*

Long-Burning Baked Oats

Prep: about forty-five minutes
Ready in one hour and fifteen minutes

This was a well-enjoyed recipe I provided in *Your Worthy Body*. While it's not difficult, it takes a bit of time to make, but you'll have plenty to enjoy for snacks, breakfasts, and even to share.

Just about everything in here is a nutrient-dense complex carb, so you'll get plenty of micronutrient superpower with this one!

Ingredients

- 4 cups rolled (old-fashioned) oats (gluten-free if necessary)
- 1 tsp baking powder
- 2 tsp cinnamon
- ¼ tsp salt
- ¼ cup honey
- ¼ cup unsalted butter, melted and slightly cooled
- 2 ripe medium bananas, mashed
- 1 large egg
- ¾ cup pumpkin puree
- 1 cup milk, your choice
- 1 Granny Smith apple, diced
- 1 cup matchstick carrots, cut into smaller sticks (½-inch in length)
- 3 oz. 70% dark chocolate bar, chopped
- 1 cup walnuts, chopped (optional)

Instructions

Preheat the oven to 350 degrees. Spray a 13 x 9 baking pan with nonstick spray. In a medium bowl, mix oats, baking powder, cinnamon, and salt. Set aside.

In a separate bowl, combine mashed bananas, egg, honey, pumpkin puree, and milk. Then add melted butter (this prevents the heated butter from slightly cooking the egg).

Combine the dry ingredients with the wet ingredients. Add in apple, carrots, chocolate, and walnuts. Pour and pat into the baking pan. Bake for thirty-five minutes. Let cool for five minutes before serving.

Store extras in the refrigerator or freezer, not on the counter. I cut the pan into squares and put half into the fridge for the week. I individually wrap the other half in plastic wrap and freeze them for later. My recipe testers and I learned the hard way that if you leave the bars on the counter, they get moldy. Ew.

Breakfast Cookies

Adapted from Sara Snow

Prep: about fifteen minutes

These have been a breakfast staple for over fifteen years at my house. They are quick to make, and I often double the recipe and freeze half.

When I found this recipe, Sara called these "Energy-Sustaining Breakfast Bars." Let's be honest—that doesn't sell. Cookies for breakfast? That sells.

Ingredients

- 2 1/2 cups old-fashioned oats (gluten-free if necessary)
- 1/2 cup ground flax seed
- 1/4 cup dark cocoa powder (or slightly less)
- 1/2 cup honey
- 1/2–1 cup HOT water
- 1/2 cup natural peanut butter

Directions

Prepare by cutting wax paper into 6 x 6-inch (-ish) squares.

> **Pro Tip:** *First, pull out wax paper into foot-long sections so you have about one square foot. Do this three times. Then, cut each foot into quarters so each square is about 6 x 6 inches. For all you perfectionists out there, be flexible. They won't be perfect squares, and that's okay. We just need to be able to wrap the finished cookies.*

Stir together the dry ingredients (oats through cocoa powder) until well mixed. Add in the honey and hot water and stir well. You just need enough water to wet everything together (we aren't making soup or runny oatmeal!).

Add in the peanut butter and mix until well blended.

Form into individual sized patties, like hamburgers. Use your hands or a cookie batter scoop.

Place in wax paper bags or plastic wrap and keep in the refrigerator. If you double the recipe, store the wrapped cookies in a freezer-safe Ziploc bag.

> **Disclaimer:** *I did not say these were pretty. In fact, they may remind you of our topic of conversation in Chapter 29. But have a couple of these in the morning and you will, in fact, find you have sustaining energy.*

Acknowledgments

Writing may be a solo act, but it takes a team of people to create a book.

To my teen clients: Thank you for trusting me with your bodies. And for those of you who showed up outside in the middle of summer, you rock. I learned more from you than you know.

To the early readers: Whether you provided feedback from *Your Worthy Body* or were an early reader for *Your CORE Strength*, I appreciate your time and honest words. You are so wise! Thank you to Meredith B., Ella C., Milea C., Amelie G., Anna G., Julia H., Liviya M., Meredith M., and Natalie O.

To the creatives: You took my words and created a visual, tangible work of art. Thank you Steve Kuhn (interior and exterior design), Erin Bartles (marketing copy), and Katherine Suzette (headshots).

To my editor: Meaghan Minkus, you're amazing. Who else could have corrected so many commas and also been the diet culture police? No one, that's who. Also thank you for your flexibility and grace with the last-minute changes.

To Wingerd Media: It's always a joy to work with you. Who knew I could mess up so much reading my own words? Thank you for creating the audio version of Your CORE Strength to reach readers in a different way.

To Lenae Bulthuis: I could not have written this without your wisdom, guidance, and encouragement. God's mighty hand was at work when he connected us through our friend Cheri Fletcher (thank you, Cheri, for the introduction and so much more!).

To Leslie Schilling: I asked for the diet culture police and got the diet culture head of the FBI. Your time spent going through this with a fine-tooth comb helped make this a safe space. Thank you!

To my family: We made it through another one! You know all the ways you've supported me in this project. Thank you.

To Jesus: You get the glory on this one. Thank You for connecting me with this incredible team and for giving me the right words and message. I pray it honors You, Your Word, and Your heart for all of us.

NOTES

Chapter 3

1. Billy Hawkins, Raegan A. Tuff, and Gary Dudley, "African American Women, Body Composition, and Physical Activity," *Journal of African American Studies* 10 (2006), https://doi.org/10.1007/s12111-006-1012-5.

2. Vanessa Van Edwards, "Beauty Standards: See How Body Types Change Through History," Science of People, accessed July 10, 2020, https://www.scienceofpeople.com/beauty-standards/.

Chapter 4

1. "Loneliness Statistics," SocialSelf, accessed September 23, 2003, https://socialself.com/loneliness-statistics/#2.

2. "Loneliness Comparable to Smoking Up to 15 Cigarettes a Day," *Fortune*, June 15, 2023, https://fortune.com/well/2023/06/15/loneliness-comparable-to-smoking-up-to-15-cigarettes-a-day/.

Chapter 7

1. Malini Ghoshal, "What You Need to Know About Set Point Theory," Healthline, March 19, 2020, https://www.healthline.com/health/set-point-theory.html.

2. Sara Berg, MS, "AMA: Use of BMI alone is an imperfect clinical measure," June 14, 2023, https://www.ama-assn.org/delivering-care/public-health/ama-use-bmi-alone-imperfect-clinical-measure.

3. "10 Ways Sleep Deprivation Affects Your Health," Cleveland Clinic, August 23, 2019, https://health.clevelandclinic.org/10-ways-sleep-deprivation-affects-your-health/.

4. Hedy Marks, "Stress Symptoms," WebMD, October 8, 2023, https://www.webmd.com/balance/stress-management/stress-symptoms-effects_of-stress-on-the-body.

5. "What causes amenorrhea?" National Institutes of Health, January 31, 2017, https://www.nichd.nih.gov/health/topics/amenorrhea/conditioninfo/causes.

Chapter 8

1. Sanjay Gupta, *Keep Sharp* (New York: Simon & Schuster, 2021), 132.

2. Simon N. Young, "How to increase serotonin in the human brain without drugs," *Journal of Psychiatry and Neuroscience*, vol. 32 (November 2007): https://www.ncbi.nlm.nih.gov/pmc/articles/PMC2077351/.

3. Andrew Huberman, "Using Light (Sunlight, Blue Light & Red Light) to Optimize Health," *The Huberman Lab*, April 18, 2022, https://www.hubermanlab.com/episode/using-light-sunlight-blue-light-and-red-light-to-optimize-health.

4. Kelly McGonigal, *The Joy of Movement* (New York: Avery Publishing, 2019), 53.

5. Andrew Huberman, "The Effects of Cannabis (Marijuana) on the Brain & Body," *The Huberman Lab*, October 3, 2022, https://www.hubermanlab.com/episode/the-effects-of-cannabis-marijuana-on-the-brain-and-body.

6. Andrew Huberman, "What Alcohol Does to Your Body, Brain & Health," *The Huberman Lab*, August 22, 2022, https://www.hubermanlab.com/episode/what-alcohol-does-to-your-body-brain-health.

Chapter 9

1. "Effects of caffeine on anxiety and panic attacks in patients with panic disorder: A systematic review and meta-analysis," *General Hospital Psychiatry* January-February 2022, https://pubmed.ncbi.nlm.nih.gov/34871964/.

2. "What Is Box Breathing?" WebMD, April 30, 2023, https://www.webmd.com/balance/what-is-box-breathing.

3. Jacob Stern, "Something Weird Is Going On With Melatonin," *The Atlantic*, May 18, 2023, https://www.theatlantic.com/health/archive/2023/05/melatonin-kids-overdose/674104/.

Chapter 10

1. Vivienne M. Hazzard et. al., "Food Insecurity and Eating Disorders: A Review of Emerging Evidence," *Current Psychiatry Reports* 22, no. 12 (October 30, 2020): 74, https://www.ncbi.nlm.nih.gov/pmc/articles/PMC7596309/.

2. "Understanding the Stress Response," *Harvard Health Journal*, July 6, 2020, https://www.health.harvard.edu/staying-healthy/understanding-the-stress-response.

Chapter 11

1. Erin Nitschke, "5 Ways to Ditch Diet Culture," American Council on Exercise, September 16, 2022, https://www.acefitness.org/resources/everyone/blog/8151/5-ways-to-ditch-diet-culture-for-good/.

2. Christy Harrison, *Anti-Diet: Reclaim Your Time, Money, Well-Being, and Happiness through Intuitive Eating* (New York: Little, Brown Spark 2019), 3.

3. Malini Ghoshal, "What You Need to Know About Set Point Theory," Healthline, March 19, 2020, https://www. healthline.com/health/set-point-theory.html.

4. Vivienne M. Hazzard et. al., "Food Insecurity and Eating Disorders: A Review of Emerging Evidence," *Current Psychiatry Reports* 22, no. 12 (October 30, 2020): 74, https://www.ncbi.nlm.nih.gov/pmc/articles/PMC7596309/.

5. "Understanding the Stress Response," *Harvard Health Journal*, July 6, 2020, https://www.health.harvard.edu/staying-healthy/understanding-the-stress-response.

6. Leslie Schilling, *Feed Yourself* (Grand Rapids, Michigan: Zondervan Books, 2023), 208.

Chapter 12

1. Merriam-Webster, s.v. "nutrient (n.)," accessed November 3, 2023, https://www.merriam-webster.com/dictionary/nutrient.

2. Angela Weyand et. al., "Prevalence of Iron Deficiency and Iron-Deficiency Anemia in US Females Aged 12-21 Years, 2003-2020," *JAMA Network* (June 27, 2023): https://jamanetwork.com/journals/jama/fullarticle/2806540.

3. Linda Carroll, "Why symptoms of iron deficiency are often missed in young women and girls," NBC News, July 1, 2023, https://www.nbcnews.com/health/health-news/iron-deficiency-often-missed-young-women-girls-research-finds-rcna92046.

Chapter 13

1. Dictionary.com, s.v. "nourish (v.)," accessed August 1, 2021, https://www.dictionary.com/browse/nourish.

Chapter 14

1. B. Benelam et. al., "Hydration and health: a review," *Nutrition Bulletin* (February 22, 2010): https://onlinelibrary.wiley.com/doi/full/10.1111/j.1467-3010.2009.01795.x.

2. Lisa Drayer, "Sparkling Water vs. Still Water: Is One Better for Your Health?" CNN, July 19, 2018, https://www.cnn.com/2018/07/19/health/sparkling-water-hydration-drayer/index.html.

Chapter 15

1. Gavin Van de Walle, "9 Important Functions of Protein in the Body," Healthline, February 15, 2023, https://www.healthline.com/nutrition/functions-of-protein.

2. Fabio Comona, "The Second Scoop on Protein: When, What and How Much?" NASM, accessed September 27, 2023, https://blog.nasm.org/fitness/the-second-scoop-on-protein-when-what-and-how-much.

3. Stephan van Vliet et. al., "Achieving Optimal Post-Exercise Muscle Protein Remodeling in Physically Active Adults through Whole Food Consumption," *Nutrients* (February 2018): https://pubmed.ncbi.nlm.nih.gov/29462924/.

4. Tim Snijders et. al., "The Impact of Pre-sleep Protein Ingestion on the Skeletal Muscle Adaptive Response to Exercise in Humans: An Update," *Frontiers in Nutrition* (March 6, 2019): https://www.ncbi.nlm.nih.gov/pmc/articles/PMC6415027/.

Chapter 16

1. Arne Arnstrup et. al., "Saturated Fats and Health: A Reassessment and Proposal for Food-Based Recommendations: JACC State-of-the-Art Review," *Journal of the American College of Cardiology* (August 2020): https://www.jacc.org/doi/abs/10.1016/j.jacc.2020.05.077.

2. "Trans Fat," Food & Drug Administration, August 30, 2023, https://www.fda.gov/food/food-additives-petitions/trans-fat.

Chapter 17

1. Pierre J. Majistretti et. al., "A Cellular Perspective on Brain Energy Metabolism and Functional Imaging," *Neuron* 86, May 20, 2015: 883-901, https://www.cell.com/neuron/pdf/S0896-6273(15)00259-7.pdf.
2. Julie E. Holesh et. al., "Physiology, Carbohydrates," *StatPearls*, May 12, 2023, https://www.ncbi.nlm.nih.gov/books/NBK459280/.
3. "The Liver & Blood Sugar," Diabetes Education Online, Diabetes Teaching Center at the University of California, San Francisco, accessed December 19, 2023, https://dtc.ucsf.edu/types-of-diabetes/type1/understanding-type-1-diabetes/how-the-body-processes-sugar/the-liver-blood-sugar/.
4. Kristeen Cherney, "Simple Carbohydrates vs. Complex Carbohydrates," Healthline, updated May 10, 2023, https://www.healthline.com/health/food-nutrition/simple-carbohydrates-complex-carbohydrates.

Chapter 18

1. "Insulin," Cleveland Clinic, March 7, 2022, https://my.clevelandclinic.org/health/body/22601-insulin.
2. "Added Sugars," American Heart Association, last reviewed November 21, 2021, https://www.heart.org/en/healthy-living/healthy-eating/eat-smart/sugar/added-sugars.

Chapter 19

1. Denise Webb, "Farewell to the 3,500-Calorie Rule," *Today's Dietitian*, November 2014, https://www.todaysdietitian.com/newarchives/111114p36.shtml.
2. Simone Seitz, "Disordered Eating as a Precursor to Eating Disorders," *NEDA Blog*, October 29, 2018, https://www.nationaleatingdisorders.org/blog/disordered-eating-precursor-eating-disorders.
3. Aaron Flores, RDN, "What does Intuitive Eating Mean?" *NEDA Blog*, March 2, 2018, https://www.nationaleatingdisorders.org/blog/what-does-intuitive-eating-mean.

Chapter 23

1. Zachary Mang, MS et. al., "Metabolic Effects of Resistance Training," *IDEA Fitness Journal* 16(5) (2019): 20-29, https://www.unm.edu/~lkravitz/Article%20folder/metaboliceffectsofRT.html.

Chapter 29

1. "Report Offers New Eating and Physical Activity Targets To Reduce Chronic Disease Risk," The National Academy of Medicine, September 5, 2002, https://www.nationalacademies.org/news/2002/09/report-offers-new-eating-and-physical-activity-targets-to-reduce-chronic-disease-risk.
2. Mayo Clinic Staff, "Dietary fiber: Essential for a Healthy Diet," Mayo Clinic, November 4,

2022, https://www.mayoclinic.org/healthy-lifestyle/nutrition-and-healthy-eating/in-depth/fiber/art-20043983.

3. Megan Clapp et. al., "Gut microbiota's effect on mental health: The gut-brain axis," *Clinics and Practice* 7(4) (September 15, 2017): 987, https://www.ncbi.nlm.nih.gov/pmc/articles/PMC5641835/.

Chapter 30

1. Kevin D. Hall, et. al., "Maintenance of lost weight and long-term management of obesity," *Medical Clinics of North America* 102(1) (January 2018): 183–197, https://www.ncbi.nlm.nih.gov/pmc/articles/PMC5764193/.

2. "Guidance for Industry: Guide for Developing and Using Data Bases for Nutrition Labeling," U.S. Food and Drug Administration, March 1998, https://www.fda.gov/regulatory-information/search-fda-guidance-documents/guidance-industry-guide-developing-and-using-data-bases-nutrition-labeling.

3. Rob Newsom and Kimberly Truong, "Weight Loss and Sleep," Sleep Foundation, December 16, 2022, https://www.sleepfoundation.org/physical-health/weight-loss-and-sleep.

4. Marco La Marra et. al., "Using Smartphones When Eating Increases Caloric Intake in Young People: An Overview of the Literature," *Frontiers in Psychology* (Dec. 3, 2020): https://www.ncbi.nlm.nih.gov/pmc/articles/PMC7744612/.

5. Dan Buettner, "Reverse Engineering Longevity," Blue Zones, accessed December 5, 2023, https://www.bluezones.com/2016/11/power-9/.

Chapter 33

1. "11 Facts About Body Image," DoSomething.org, accessed September 23, 2023, https://www.dosomething.org/us/facts/11-facts-about-body-image.

Conclusion

1. Richard Batts, "Why Most New Year's Resolutions Fail," The Ohio State University Fisher College of Business, February 2, 2023, https://fisher.osu.edu/blogs/leadreadtoday/why-most-new-years-resolutions-fail.

2. Katharina Buchholz, "America's Top New Year's Resolutions for 2023," Statista, December 23, 2022, https://www.statista.com/chart/29019/most-common-new-years-resolutions-us/.

www.ingramcontent.com/pod-product-compliance
Lightning Source LLC
Chambersburg PA
CBHW052134070526
44585CB00017B/1823